The Story of Baseball

The story of baseball is packed with unforgettable moments, colorful personalities, explosive rivalries and feuds, tense pennant races and World Series. In this lively book, generously illustrated with photographs, John Rosenburg recalls the prominent highlights of this exciting game, tracing the gradual growth and development of major-league baseball through the past hundred years.

Random House New York

The Story of Baseball

By John M. Rosenburg

Illustrated with photographs

Who, above all, should know the stirring tales of the great Ruth and Johnson, DiMaggio and Feller? Who, but the young of today... and the young of all the tomorrows?

While this book, then, was written for boys and girls everywhere, I dedicate it with deepest affection to one youngster in particular—my son, John J., who was twelve when the manuscript was completed.

Acknowledgments

It took about three years to complete the manuscript for *The Story of Baseball*. Naturally, when the last period was struck, I was quite pleased with myself. And yet I realized full well that I could not possibly have assembled so much material and sustained my efforts over so long a period without a great deal of assistance. I would like, therefore, to express my deepest appreciation for this wealth of invaluable aid, which came from many sources and in many forms.

I am especially grateful to the hundreds of sports-loving writers who, for more than a century, so carefully and enthusiastically chronicled the birth and growth of baseball. Without their works to draw from, I could not have established the foundation for this book.

While I read some 35 books covering various aspects of baseball, as well as scores of magazines and newspaper articles, I found the following to be the most helpful:

Baseball by Robert Smith; *America's National Game* by A. G. Spalding; *A Ball Player's Career* by Adrian Constantine Anson; *100 Years of Baseball* and *Hot Stove League* by Lee Allen; *General "Baseball" Doubleday* by Robert S. Holzman; *Ball, Bat and Bishop* by Robert W. Henderson; *Richter's History and Records of Baseball* by Francis C. Richter; *The Babe and I* by Mrs. George Herman Ruth; *Connie Mack* by Fred Lieb; *The Real McGraw* by Mrs. John McGraw; *Baseball's Famous First Basemen* and *Baseball's Famous Pitchers* by Ira Smith; *Gas House Gang and a Couple of Other Guys* by Roy Stockton; *The Yankee Story* by Tom Meany; *Baseball* by Harold Seymour; *The History of Baseball* by Allison Danzig and Joe Reichler.

Source material, of course, is but one of the props a writer must lean on as he labors to put a book-length story together. From a variety of people he needs advice and counsel, coöperation, an understanding of a journalist's problems, and even such things as top-flight typing and proof-reading help. Above all, he needs encouragement.

On all of these counts, I was most fortunate. At the outset, for example, I was lucky enough to receive direction and guidance from Lee Allen, historian of the National Baseball Hall of Fame. And as the manuscript grew, Richard G. Harris, a longtime friend—and a writer and editor of uncommon ability—went over my work and made a number of important suggestions.

During my long experience as a sports writer, however, I learned that prose style alone does not endear one to the baseball fan—a fellow who wants all the key facts and figures and wants them to be correct. In addition, the flavor of any incident under discussion has to be just so. To cover myself in this area, I imposed on two people I can best identify —and with some pride—as baseball fans. The genuine kind. They are Messrs. Frank Dugan and Frank Pacifico.

To all of these gentlemen and to the several others who contributed to this modest effort, I again give my thanks.

J.M.R.

The Story of Baseball

EXCITEMENT IN MILWAUKEE

Late one beautiful afternoon in October of 1957, Mayor Frank Zeidler of Milwaukee rushed out of his office at City Hall and raced to the building's bell tower. Grasping the bell rope, he tugged away lustily.

As five deep *bongs* from the great bell rolled across the city, people of all descriptions poured across sidewalks and into the streets. Bringing traffic to a tangled standstill, they screamed, cheered, sang, pounded each other on the back, and shouted over and over:

"We did it!" "We did it!"

Hundreds of automobile horns, seemingly stuck, and scores of shrieking factory whistles added to the din. In the suburbs, fire sirens let loose wail after wail, although there were no fires and the fire engines remained where they were.

When the Mayor left the bell tower, he announced that all city employees were—from that moment—on holiday. Suddenly realizing he was included in the order, the Mayor seized a flag, ran into the streets, and started an impromptu parade.

Flags, signs, confetti, and colored streamers fluttered in the breezes everywhere. At least a hundred banners carried the words:

"Burdette for President. Mathews for Vice President."

3

Lew Burdette is congratulated by his teammates.

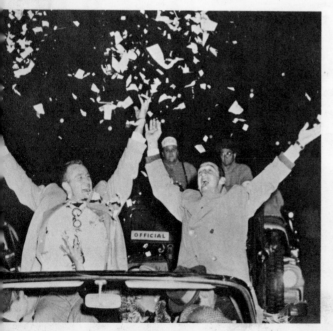

Lew Burdette (left) and Warren Spahn toss out the pieces of paper thrown into their car during Milwaukee's welcome-home celebration for the Braves.

Four Winnebago Indian maidens, in full native costume, cavorted on one street corner to give the sudden eruption of activity an even more colorful note.

What was the excitement about?

A baseball team—the Milwaukee Braves of the National League—had defeated the New York Yankees of the American League by a score of 5-0 in the seventh and deciding game of a World Series.

When the Braves flew into Milwaukee from New York that night (escorted by a group of Wisconsin National Guard jet fighters), they touched off the greatest celebration in the city's history.

Debarking from their plane, they walked across a 50-foot red carpet to a caravan of waiting automobiles. Some 400,000 persons lined the route the cars followed as they moved slowly from the airport to the heart of the city. (The total population of Milwaukee at the time was 638,000.)

The unbounded joy that swept Milwaukee in the fall of 1957 (and the contrasting gloom that pervaded New York, hometown of the Yankees) is nothing new to Americans. It's the sort of thing that happens every year at World Series time.

A stranger to the United States might well wonder at this state of affairs.

"After all," he could be expected to say, "it's only a *game.*"

But baseball is more than a mere game to most Americans. It's a National Pastime. And here is the story of how this came about.

1. A New Game for a New Country

In a single baseball season, as many as 35 or 40 million spectators pay admission to sit in ball parks, where they watch professional or amateur players battle for team honors. Many millions of additional fans follow the games by radio and television. And another 10 million adults and boys participate in organized amateur baseball programs that are not in any way connected with public or private schools.

When one thinks about the enormous popularity of baseball, a pertinent question often comes to mind:

Where did this great national game begin?

Actually the origins of baseball are somewhat hazy. Except for box scores, very little about baseball was recorded before 1900. A great many people insist that baseball is a purely American game invented in 1839 by Abner Doubleday in Cooperstown, New York. Others argue that baseball evolved from the British games of rounders and cricket. The controversy was at its hottest during the early 1900s.

One of the earliest champions of the rounders theory was Henry Chadwick. Born in England in 1824, Chadwick moved to the United States when he was just thirteen years old. Six years later he began a remarkable writing career, covering baseball games for the biggest newspapers and magazines of his day. He also wrote books about baseball for boys and girls, originated the baseball scoring system, compiled the first rule book, and made many other suggestions.

Because he was such an authority, many people referred to Chadwick as the "Father of Baseball." But Chadwick, of all people, refused to agree that baseball originated in America. "The similarity of baseball and rounders is fully identified," he said. "And rounders was played in England two centuries before its appearance in America."

The rounders theory is supported by two books. The first one, *The Boy's Own Book,* was published in London in 1829. In it appeared the rules for rounders. The second book, *The Boy's and Girl's Book of Sports*, was published in America in 1835. The author of the second book obviously copied the first book when describing the rules of the game. But he didn't call it rounders. Instead the game was identified as Base or Goal Ball.

Albert Goodwill Spalding, one of professional baseball's founding fathers, refused to go along with the rounders theory. In fact he called it sheer nonsense. And he formed a committee of baseball notables to settle "once and for all" the matter of baseball's origins. Abraham G. Mills, former president of the National League, was chairman. The group labored for three years before reaching, in 1907, a twofold decision. Baseball had its origin, they announced, in the United States. The first scheme for playing baseball was devised by Abner Doubleday at Cooperstown in 1839.

Who was this Abner Doubleday? And on what had the Mills Commission based its findings?

Doubleday, dead at the time the report was issued, was a well-known Union Army general. He was also a friend of Mills. His name had been brought to the attention of the Commission by Abner Graves, a mining engineer who lived in Denver, Colorado. In a letter to the Commission, Graves said he had gone to school with Doubleday at Coop-

Even if Abner Doubleday didn't invent baseball, the Union general did distinguish himself at the Battle of Gettysburg.

erstown. And he recalled seeing Doubleday organize a game called "Base Ball, for there were four bases in it . . ." Graves gave the year as 1839. And he implied that Doubleday had been disturbed by the fact that a ball game he and others were playing was badly organized and permitted too many players to compete. Doubleday, according to Graves, cut down the number of players and suggested the game be played between competing teams.

Although the Mills Commission seized on the letter as "evidence," most historians now reject it. They point out that Graves was more than 80 years old when he wrote the letter. He very likely would not have been able to recall accurately what had gone on so many years earlier. It was also noted that Doubleday could not have been in Cooperstown in 1839, for his military records show he was at West Point. In addition, Doubleday wrote several books and left a mountain of papers to his heirs. Nowhere did he mention baseball.

It now seems more likely that baseball evolved gradually into the game we know today. American boys and girls of the early 1800s were surely just as inventive as today's young players. Starting with the game of rounders or Base ball, they no doubt changed the official rules to suit the conditions under which the game was played. Thus there developed such games as one old cat and two old cat (using one and two bases). Then came town ball, with four bases and a batter's box between home base and first base.

All of these were variations on the

same principle. A ball was tossed to a batter. The batter hit the ball and ran to a base, or bases. The equipment and the methods of scoring and putting out runners or batters varied. One big difference between town ball and the other games was that the players were young men instead of children. In addition to whacking the ball with a bat, these older players took great delight in "soaking" or "stinging" base runners with the thrown ball.

Town ball—with its many variations— reached the height of its popularity in the early 1800s. It proved to be an excellent source of recreation in a world where automobiles, radios, and television sets were not even dreamed of. There was plenty of space in which to play, and equipment was cheap. Best of all, any red-blooded male could compete.

Soon the town-ball players began to form clubs. And the formation of the clubs represented the first step toward the game of professional baseball as we know it today.

2. The Gentlemen Players

For the most part, the first of the clubs organized solely for the purpose of playing "base ball" had as members young men who came from the wealthier branches of society. These high-born "gentlemen" played for exercise and a spot of fun. Most of them had played cricket, an English game that was very popular in America at the time. Though they found base ball more exciting, they still retained the genteel manners and sportsmanship of the cricket players.

The most famous ball-playing group of the early 1800s was the Knickerbocker Club of New York City. This organization enjoyed baseball immensely. The members met two or three times a week—first in Manhattan, then just across the Hudson River in New Jersey, where there was more room. The Knickerbockers soon realized that there was one great weakness to their favorite game—a lack of standard rules. To correct this fault, the officers of the club appointed a committee to draw up a set of rules and make copies for every member.

One of the committeemen was a six-foot, 200-pound player named Alexander Joy Cartwright, Jr. Cartwright, one of the club's best players, is generally given credit for getting the rules formulated and published. And because many of these rules include principles contained in today's regulations, Cartwright is often referred to as "The Father of Baseball."

The committee seems to have been the first to establish the baseball diamond by ruling that:

"The bases shall be from 'home' to second base, 42 paces, from first to third base, 42 paces, equidistant."

The principle of innings, with each team going to bat in turn, is embodied in the second Knickerbocker rule:

According to the rules of the New England Game, a base runner was out if hit by a thrown ball.

"The game shall consist of 21 counts or aces, but at the end *an equal number of hands* [innings] *must be played.*"

The third rule required that the ball "must be pitched, not thrown for the bat."

Other rules provided that a ball knocked outside the range of first or third base was foul. A player running the bases was out if the ball was in the hands of an opponent on the base, and the runner was touched by it before he reached the base. In no instance, however, was the ball to be thrown at him. When three players were out, all were out.

Players were to take their bat in regular turn. No base or ace—as they called a run—could be made on a foul strike. All disputes and differences related to the game were to be decided by the umpire, from whose decision there was no appeal.

The rules made two other points: they set the pitching distance at 45 feet and, apparently for the first time, limited each team to nine players.

Although baseball rules have undergone many, many changes through the years, they have always included better than half of the original Knickerbocker regulations, even if the wording has changed somewhat.

When the Cartwright committee, after many hours of intensive work, finally showed the first draft of the new rules to fellow club members, the Knickerbocker meeting place rang with shouted suggestions. Here was something new, something different, and something terribly exciting.

Finally the club president, Duncan F. Curry, quieted the members down. After a long, animated discussion, it was decided that the Knicks would invite a "nine" from the New York Club to play a match game at the Elysian Field in Hoboken, New Jersey, a short ferry ride from Manhattan. The game would be played under the newly written rules, and the loser would pay for a banquet at McCarty's Hotel, situated near the field. Alexander Cartwright was chosen to act as umpire.

The Knicks set the date for June 19, 1846, and the New York club promptly accepted the challenge. The first match game of record was on!

One of the early baseball games played at the Elysian Field in Hoboken, N. J.

The Knicks were so confident of victory they didn't bother to practice for the game. They were in for a surprise. The opposing pitcher—a well-known cricket bowler—whipped a little six-ounce ball with a rubber center past the Knick batters inning after inning. The Knicks got just one run. The New York team, meanwhile, scored 23 runs! Though the Knicks lost at their own game, the defeat was quickly forgotten at McCarty's Hotel, where a spirit of good fellowship and sportsmanship prevailed.

During the course of the game, Umpire Cartwright fined one of the players six cents "for cussin'." The club rules didn't permit such a thing, for baseball was a gentlemen's game. It wasn't to remain that way for long.

11

3. The Will to Win

The New York Nine either went back to cricket or disbanded, for the team never played the Knickerbockers again. As a matter of fact, the Knicks were unable to find another opponent for five years. Then suddenly, in the 1850s, organized clubs began to spring up everywhere—in New York, Philadelphia, Boston, Baltimore, Washington, D.C., and virtually every large eastern city. Although the Knicks had many requests for copies of their rules, some areas stubbornly held out against adopting them. As a result there developed the Philadelphia game, the Massachusetts game and, of course, the New York game, which was the Knickerbocker version.

As the years slipped by, the make-up of teams changed. The clubs were no longer limited to "gentlemen." Clerks, shopkeepers, accountants—almost any young man who could find the time— joined "the nines."

By the late 1850s well over 200 clubs had been organized. But there was constant bickering about the rules. In 1857 sixteen clubs formed the National Organization of Base Ball Players to establish a uniform playing code. One rule among those finally adopted was very important. It said members *could not accept money* for playing baseball.

The Civil War—which lasted from 1861 to 1865—hampered the activities of the National Organization, but it did much to popularize baseball. Union and Confederate soldiers played the game to keep fit and while away idle time. The game also found favor with prisoners of both armies. Sometimes the prisoners played against their captors.

Following the war, any young man worthy of his name had to sport a beard and play baseball. Teams formed at a faster rate than ever and heated rivalries began to grow between clubs representing different towns and communities.

Slowly the burning desire of teams to build a long string of victories spoiled the completely amateur status of the game. To get around the rule prohibiting direct payments, managers found jobs in factories or offices for the better players. The club members either didn't work at all at these jobs or at best worked only part time. The salaries they received were definitely for playing baseball.

One of the most famous of the post-Civil War teams—sometimes called "Muffin Nines"—was made up of players who worked for the federal government in Washington, D.C. This team, officially known as the Nationals, was probably the first to go on tour. A great crowd, cheering lustily and waving banners, saw the players off at Washington's Union Station.

They traveled a total of 2,400 miles by rail, boat, wagon, and horseback—a tremendous accomplishment for that day. In the space of about three weeks the Nationals played ten games, winning nine, some by such scores as 113–26, 106–21 and 88–12!

Their lone defeat came at the hands

of a club no one had heard much about. It was a team representing the little town of Rockford, Illinois. The pitcher for the Rockford nine—a tall, handsome, and powerful teen-ager named Albert Goodwill Spalding—had much to do with his team's victory. Spalding, to the amazement of all who saw or heard about the game, held the powerful Nationals to 23 runs, while the Rockford stalwarts scored 29.

The intense interest that people were showing in these games soon prompted newspapers and sporting magazines to report on the events. Some publications even assigned writers to travel with the principal teams when they were on tour. Naturally the reporting of games in the nation's newspapers and periodicals greatly heightened interest in baseball. As interest grew, so did the urge to win. These twin elements soon brought about a major change in baseball. It continued to be an amateur sport, but it also became a business. Its popularity was rapidly increasing.

4. The Brothers Wright

In the spring of 1866, Harry Wright, a muscular man of average build, left New York for Cincinnati. Wright was moving to the thriving Ohio city to take a job in a sports club as a cricket professional. Like the professional at today's golf clubs, Wright was to give lessons to members, arrange matches, and in general do what he could to stimulate interest in cricket.

Wright wasn't at the sports club very long before he discovered that the good citizens of Cincinnati were not much interested in cricket. Like hundreds of Americans in other cities, they had taken a liking to baseball.

This didn't pose too much of a problem for Wright. He knew as much about baseball as anyone. He and his brothers —Sam and George Wright—had played baseball as well as cricket. In no time at all, Harry Wright organized a ball team for the club. It was called the Red Stockings. Wright himself pitched, played center field, and managed the team.

He soon discovered a tough opponent in another Cincinnati nine, the Buckeyes. One season of play made him realize that the Red Stockings would need better players if they were to make a good showing against the Buckeyes and other strong teams. During the winter Wright contacted three players he knew in the East. He promised them good jobs in Cincinnati if they would join his Red Stockings. The trio accepted and, along with Wright, formed the heart of the Red Stocking team that took the field in 1868. It must have been a good team. The Buckeyes were beaten so badly and so often by the Red Stockings that they disbanded. But for the Red Stockings the 1868 season was only the beginning.

Wright's success with the three imported players set him to thinking. Why not bring in enough players to fill every position? And why not pay these players *directly* instead of pretending to place them in jobs? A salary for playing ball would have great appeal for players, Wright reasoned. It would also give the manager a better hold on them.

The more Wright thought about this idea the better he liked it, even though such a thing was unheard of at the time. Finally he made up his mind. He would write several good players and offer them a fair salary for joining the Red Stockings.

All through the off-season, Wright corresponded with ball players. One of them was his brother George, who had been playing with the Washington Nationals. By the spring of 1869, Wright had his team assembled. And when the Red Stockings took the field that year they became America's first professional baseball team.

It was a great team, too. In 65 games during that first season the Red Stockings were undefeated. Most of the games were played while the team was on a 12,000-mile tour, the longest taken by any ball team up to that time. By the season's end the Red Stockings had played before some 200,000 fans, another remarkable achievement.

The star of the team was undoubtedly George Wright, who received $1,400 for the season. Although not a large man, George had wonderful coördination. He was good at every sport. He was so skillful with bat and ball that he often put on juggling exhibitions before game

time. It was George Wright who introduced the "pepper" game to baseball, a form of batting and fielding practice still in use.

George's play at his shortstop position brought plenty of "ooh's" and "aah's" from the fans. He was the first of the "roving" shortstops. While others played an almost stationary position to the right of the pitcher, George roamed the base line between second and third base. Crowds screamed with delight whenever he scampered in or out to snag the "bounding rock" and fire it to first base to retire a runner.

George was at his best during the famous Red Stocking tour. Playing in 52 games, he batted .518, scoring 339 times. Among his hits were 59 home runs.

Harry Wright guided the Red Stockings to another good season in 1870. By the middle of June, the team had stretched its winning streak to 80 games. The hard-fighting Atlantics of Brooklyn handed them their first defeat—8 to 7 in 11 innings before a record crowd of some 20,000.

The Red Stockings lost but five other games that year, two of them to the up-and-coming Chicago White Stockings.

But the Red Stockings—so skillfully put together and directed by Harry Wright—didn't last. Financial difficulties caused the club to disband. Soon Wright, his brother George, and a player named Gould moved to Boston, where they built another powerful team.

Harry Wright remained in baseball for many years and managed many winning teams. During these years he was constantly quoted in newspapers and

The championship Boston team organized by the Wright brothers in the 1870s. Al Spalding, pitcher, is standing second from left. George and Harry Wright are seated, third and fourth from left respectively.

magazines. The things he said had a profound effect on baseball.

Time and again, for example, he stressed the fact that if fans wanted to see good baseball they should pay a fair price for a ticket to watch a game. He thought the price should be fifty cents. Others argued that it ought to be half that amount.

Wright also believed that once in the ball park, the fan was entitled to see only the best efforts of the players. In an era when athletes lived recklessly and carelessly, Wright insisted on good behavior and physical conditioning. Throughout his lifetime he was admired and respected by all who came in contact with him. But, above all, he gave the game of baseball its first big push toward professionalism. And this is a contribution which should never be overlooked.

5.   A Short, Unhappy Life

The astounding success of the Cincinnati Red Stockings in 1869 and 1870 made one thing all too clear to baseball promoters everywhere. To enjoy fame and, more important, to make money, a team must seek out the best players and pay them for their services.

Soon professional clubs began to join the National Association. But they had to fight hard to do so. The amateur members bitterly resented their intrusion. They saw many evils in the professional game. Gamblers followed the professional teams everywhere, betting openly in the stands. The players often joined in the betting. This led to corruption and dishonesty.

While the amateurs were still struggling to keep the professionals out of the National Association, a gambling scandal rocked the baseball world. It was proved that three members of the Mutuals had "thrown" a game to the Eckfords, a weaker team. The Eckfords won 28 to 11. A group of gamblers and Mutual players made a handsome profit on this dishonest bargain.

The amateurs had other complaints. They charged that the professionals flouted the rules in every way. They accused them of doing *anything* to win.

In addition, the professionals would leave one club and move to another at the slightest mention of more pay.

"Disgraceful!" the amateurs protested.

Obviously the two kinds of teams couldn't stay in the same organization. And they didn't. In the spring of 1871, representatives of ten professional teams met in New York. They formed the National Association of *Professional* Base Ball Players. The ten original members included:

The Philadelphia Athletics, Forest Cities of Rockford, Chicago White Stockings, Forest Cities of Cleveland, Boston Red Stockings, Troy Unions, New York Mutuals, Washington Olympics, Washington Nationals and the Kekiongas of Fort Wayne.

The formation of this second National Association was important for one very particular reason. The rules provided that member clubs were to play each other five times. The team winning the most games would then be considered baseball champions of the United States. This is how the first championship series was started.

The honor of winning the first pennant race went to Philadelphia. Harry Wright's Boston Red Stockings took the next four in a row.

The launching of the all-professional league and the establishment of a national championship looked wonderfully simple on paper. But these first professionals were sailing on a mighty leaky ship. Players who continually moved from one team to another caused the biggest problem. There was no legal way for the Association to make a player stay with his club. If the owner of the Athletics wanted to strengthen his team by hiring a pitcher working for the Boston Red Stockings, he simply approached the pitcher and offered him more money than he was already receiving.

Ball players didn't get much for their services. And since the playing season was short, they had a hard time indeed to earn enough to live on throughout the year. It was only natural that they should move to greener pastures whenever they could.

The owners had a money problem, too. They had to make a profit to survive. This meant they had to build a strong team and *win*. Fans have never gone to a ball park to watch a constant loser. As a result, the owners bid against each other for the better players.

By the time the Association was formed, many of the imperfections in the original Cartwright rules had been eliminated. There were still many loopholes, however, in the playing rules. The Association tried hard to correct them, for professional baseball had become a form of entertainment. To draw fans, the game had to be interesting, exciting.

The players found all sorts of ways to get around the rules. Little Dickey Pearce, a well-known shortstop in the

The Athletics play the Philadelphia Club in 1873. Note the umpire's top hat and the first baseman playing in foul ground.

1870s, harassed the opposition with a "fair-foul" hit. He would bunt the ball in such a way that it would land in fair territory, then roll into foul. Even the greenest amateur player knows that infielders have enough trouble handling a bunt that *stays* between the foul lines. To make a play on a bunt that lands in fair territory, then rolls way off into foul ground is impossible! Eventually the rulemakers were to make this particular play illegal.

Dishonesty, gambling, weak rules—all of these finally caused the collapse of America's first professional baseball organization. Another—the National League of Professional Base Ball Clubs—took its place.

6. Heroes and Heroics

Among the early players were names that will live forever. Some are known for a single feat; some became famous for years of wonderful performances; some made other contributions.

There was Al Spalding, for instance. When he pitched the Rockford nine to the stirring victory over the touring Washington team, Spalding was but 17 years old. It was a spectacular start. But it was only a start. Spalding carved an astounding career from the game he loved.

While pitching for Rockford, Spalding worked as a clerk in a grocery store at a small salary. But his strong right arm soon began to pay bigger dividends. After his first season at Rockford, he moved to Chicago to play. There he took another grocery-store job. The new position paid him $40 a week, many times his Rockford wage. The grocery failed, but Spalding returned to Rockford at the same pay.

Spalding did most of the pitching for Rockford. When the team played at home it won all but one game. This made the Rockford fans so excited they raised enough money to send the team on tour. They weren't disappointed either. For Spalding and the Rockford club again whipped the Washington Nationals. Then they defeated the openly professional Cincinnati Red Stockings.

By the time the next season rolled around, the Rockford fans decided to put an all-professional nine in the field. Spalding again joined the team. But soon Harry Wright wrote him from Boston, offering him a place on his new Red Stocking club. Spalding accepted and in his first year won 21 of 39 games. This was just the beginning. In his second year, he won 36 and lost 8. And during his last three years he won 149, averaging 49 a season! Spalding's best year was in 1875, when he won 56 and lost but five.

When Spalding and his Rockford teammates made their historic tour, one of their stops was at Marshalltown, a tiny hamlet in Iowa. The Marshalltown folk were as enthusiastic about baseball as fans in Rockford. And the nucleus of one of the very first Marshalltown teams was formed by three members of one family—the Ansons. Henry Anson, the oldest of the trio, was the father of the other two, Sturgis and Adrian.

The father played third base. Sturgis was at center field and Adrian at second base. Since Adrian was the youngest of the Ansons, he was usually referred to by fans and players as "Baby." But before he hung up his spikes and glove, Adrian was known by all baseball followers as "Pop." He was active in the big leagues for 27 years.

The Rockford promoters were so impressed with the Ansons that they offered the trio a chance to join the Rockford professional team the following season. Henry Anson declined, saying he and Sturgis had to stay in Marshalltown to tend the family business. But he gave young Adrian permission to leave home to play for Rockford.

Anson's first job as a professional ball player netted him $68 a month. But like Spalding he wasn't at Rockford long. At about the same time Spalding went to Boston, Adrian Anson joined the Philadelphia Athletics for a salary of $1,250 a year.

Anson, like Spalding, was a great player and an outstanding individual. He was courageous as a lion, fiercely honest, independent and stubborn. Anson was also opposed to drinking, gambling, and roistering. When playing ball he trained faithfully and watched his diet. On the diamond he played every game to the hilt. When he was manag-

Adrian "Cap" Anson brought fame to the Chicago White Stockings when he joined them in 1876.

ing he expected his players to play the same way.

Anson, Spalding, and the Wright brothers were but a few of the first professional players who made lasting contributions to the new game of baseball. In the 1860s Eddie Cuthbert startled the fans by sliding for a base. He did it by dropping on his seat and thrusting both legs forward. Another player, Bob Addy, was even more daring. He slid head-first, riding on his stomach.

Pitchers soon learned how to make a baseball curve. They also threw a "dew drop." This was a pitch favored by Harry Wright whenever he left his usual outfield post for the pitcher's box. It was nothing more than a slow, looping delivery intended to upset the hitter's timing. Today it is called a "change of pace."

The king of the curve-ball pitchers was tiny Arthur "Candy" Cummings. His curve was so startling that fans refused to believe it. In one game, according to an old report, 24 of the batters he faced popped the ball into the air.

In addition to developing individual skills, the early professionals added something more to the game—aggressiveness. The game became faster, more exciting. Baseball was making great strides, but it was still only a beginning.

7. Birth of the National League

After the establishment of the National Association of Professional Base Ball Players in 1871, baseball became more than just a game. It developed into a business—a big business. As such, it attracted men who had money to invest. One of these investors was William A. Hulbert, a dynamic, forceful man. Hulbert put some of his money into ownership of the Chicago White Stockings in 1875. Soon he became an official of the club.

Hulbert quickly realized that baseball could not survive if the chaotic conditions that existed under the Professional Players Association continued. Moreover, he felt the sport had to be run as a business. Along with a few friends, he set out to smash the Players Association and replace it with a stronger organization. Such a step called for strong action. And Hulbert was a strong man.

During the fall and winter of 1875–76, Hulbert maneuvered to build a new organization to replace the tottering National Association. He called to New York representatives of clubs located in eight of the choicest cities in the nation —Chicago, St. Louis, Cincinnati and Louisville in the Midwest; New York, Philadelphia, Boston and Hartford in the East.

When all were assembled, Hulbert gave each man a copy of a new league constitution. He then argued the merits of five major proposals:

1. The new organization would be a league of *clubs*, not an association of players.
2. To become members, the clubs would pay an entry fee of $100, which was 10 times what it cost to join the Players Association.

3. Only clubs operating in cities with a population of 75,000 or more would be eligible. League clubs would also have to stay at least five miles away from other clubs.

4. Players' contracts were to be written, not verbal. If a player was considered ineligible for one club, he would be ineligible for all.

5. Any player found guilty of being dishonest on the diamond was to be barred by the League for life.

While these proposals seem very simple and logical, Hulbert did not have an easy time persuading the club representatives to accept them. He cajoled, threatened, and argued from early morning until late at night. Finally the club representatives gave in to Hulbert's persuasiveness. They voted to adopt "Hulbert's Reform," as the five points came to be known. Later developments were to prove that this was one of the biggest events in baseball history.

With Morgan Bulkeley as League president, the eight clubs played a 70-game schedule. Each team played every other team five games at home and five away. All was not smooth sailing, however, during the National League's first year. Chicago was delighted with the performance of the White Stockings, but

fans in other cities lost interest in the flag race. The playing rules also continued to be a problem. The players still found ways to get around them. The power balance between pitcher and batter had not been struck, either. If the rules favored the pitcher, there were few hits and few runs. If they favored the batter, there were too many runs.

Faced with losses at the gate and a growing dissatisfaction among the fans, the club owners elected Hulbert as League president for the 1877 season. They hoped he could straighten things out.

Hulbert went right to work. He first expelled New York and Philadelphia because they had not played the full 70 games on their schedules. Thus the League started the season with six teams. It finished with even fewer. Cincinnati failed to pay its dues, so Hulbert cancelled all Cincinnati games.

In addition to his other troubles, the newspapers publicly criticized Hulbert for his dual role as president of the National League and official of the White Stockings. Many thought he was more interested in the success of the Chicago ball club than in the affairs of the League. But despite everything, the League stuck together and continued to play baseball.

8. A New Ingredient: Color

While the club owners and National League officials struggled to establish a profitable and smooth-running business, an important change was taking place on the diamond. The ball player was beginning to emerge as a national personality.

Al Spalding, of course, had been one of the first to win fame. But after his first season with the White Stockings, Spalding retired from active play. Into his place as playing manager stepped Adrian Anson.

Anson brought fame to Chicago. In his first six years as pilot of the White Stockings, the team won four pennants and never finished lower than fourth. Anson was the team's best hitter. In 20 of the 22 years he played, Anson batted .300 or better. (To bat .300 a player must average three hits out of every ten times at bat.) He ended with a lifetime average of .339, twice hitting over .400 (.407 in 1879 and .421 in 1887). Anson is one of the few players in the entire history of the game who banged out more than 3,000 hits.

Anson taught his players many new things. One of these was to shorten the grip on the bat (choke up) and hit the ball to unprotected areas (place-hit).

Along with Anson's powerful bat, the Chicago club had fine pitchers in Fred Goldsmith and Lawrence Corcoran.

And behind the plate the White Stockings had a catcher who, perhaps more than any other player of his day, electrified the fans whenever he put his foot on the diamond. He was Michael J. Kelly, whose skill at batting, running, and throwing earned him the title of "King of the Diamond." It was Kelly who discovered how to throw his flying body to one side and reach out and touch the base with the tip of a pointed toe. Kelly taught his method of sliding to his teammates and it quickly become known as "the Chicago slide." Today it is called the "hook slide," or "fadeaway."

Kelly enjoyed great popularity at Chicago. But in the biggest player deal of baseball's first decade, he was sold to Boston for $10,000. It was an unheard-of price, but Boston quickly got its money back. The Beantown fans idolized their "$10,000 Beauty," as Kelly was called. Whenever he got on base, a tremor of excitement ran through the Boston rooters. They would chant in unison: "Slide, Kelly! Slide!" Kelly rarely disappointed.

For a long time the same nine players who started a game had to finish it. But finally the League put in a substitution rule. The rule, however, proved to have a weakness, and Kelly was the one who pointed it out. During a game he was sitting on the bench while his team was on the field. A rival batter hit a pop-up that was out of reach of the regular Boston catcher. Instead, the ball came straight toward Kelly.

"Kelly now catching!" the King roared as he sprang from the bench and snared the ball. Kelly argued that the batter was out. "It's right there in the rules," he cried. "It says a substitute may enter the game *at any time*."

Kelly didn't win that argument, but the substitution rule was changed to read that a new player may enter the game only when the ball is dead (not in play). This rule still applies.

Another early star who had the appeal of Kelly and Anson was little Arlie Latham. In addition to being a skillful ball player, Latham was an expert tumbler with a delightful sense of humor. Once, as he charged to first base to beat out an

Dashing Mike Kelly in the days when he was running the Allentown, Pa., Baseball Club.

infield roller, he looked up to see Cap Anson crouching in the base line, ball in hand. Instead of slowing, or dodging, Latham kept right on. Just when a crash seemed inevitable, he took a dive right over Anson's head and landed hands-first in back of the startled first baseman. Turning a neat forward roll, he continued on.

Still another player who made a name for himself was Hugh Daily. He was a pitcher with but one arm. Daily had lost his left arm when a boy. He was burned severely in a theater fire and the arm had to be amputated. By the time he reached early manhood, however, he had thrown a baseball past some of the most feared hitters in the nation—Kelly, Anson, and George Wright.

Daily's name first appeared in headlines in 1880, when he pitched the New York Metropolitans to a 4 to 2 victory over Washington. In addition to pitching well, he knocked in the winning run with a single. During his second season with the Metropolitans, an independent team, Daily won 38 games. This was quite a record, considering the fact that he was unable to play during the month of June.

Daily, who also played the infield and outfield, eventually pitched in the National League. In 1883 he hurled a no-hit, no-run game against Philadelphia.

All of these players—Kelly, Anson, Latham, Daily, and too many more to mention—brought to baseball that indefinable quality called "color." Fans have been looking for it in ball players ever since. Luckily they always seem to find it.

9.   Baseball's First War

To stay alive through the 1870s, the National League was forced to fight a dogged, running battle on two fronts. The fracas started because William Hulbert, Harry Wright, and a few others tried to limit League membership to eight clubs and hold down player salaries. The salaries were the club owner's biggest item of expense.

Although the independent ball clubs were fairly successful—especially those with a player like Daily in the lineup—they wanted to be put on the same footing as National League teams. They also wanted to participate in the race for the "championship." It would help fill their pockets with money.

But the National League officials, on one pretense, then another, refused to admit the independents to membership.

"They've got a monopoly!" the independents cried.

To which the National Leaguers replied with a shrug, "This is the only way we can run a sound, profitable business."

While the National League owners grimly held off the independents, they struggled to control their own players and player salaries. Unfortunately a player could sell his services to any team once the season ended. Hulbert himself had lured players away from other teams, but he was among the first to recognize the danger of such a practice.

"If we constantly bid against each other for players, salaries will eventually go so high we'll all be ruined," he warned.

Hulbert had also introduced a regulation which stated that a player ineligible for one team was ineligible for all. Thus, if a player disobeyed a club's rules, he could be put on a black list. No other League team owner would hire him.

Even this wasn't enough to satisfy the owners. Hulbert and his colleagues introduced the most controversial rule baseball has ever known—the "reserve" clause.

The principle was simple: At the end of the season, each team put all of its players on a reserve list. The owners were pledged not to hire, or attempt to hire, a player on the reserve list of another team, unless the player was released.

In other words, if a player was dissatisfied with his employer, he was no longer free to move to another team. He was the property of the team to which he was under contract.

The National League's attitude angered scores of independent club owners, players, and the public. Something was bound to happen, and in the winter of 1881 it did. Alfred H. Spink, a sports writer, led a drive to form a new major league called the American Association. Charter members included the Atlantics of Brooklyn, the Alleghenys of Pittsburgh, the Athletics of Philadelphia, the Cincinnati Reds, the St. Louis Browns and the Eclipse Club of Louisville. (The Atlantics dropped out before the start of the 1882 season, and were replaced by Baltimore.)

Baseball and its questionable pleasures—as pictured in an 1883 newspaper.

What is it? — Suspected to be the Umpire

Out

Drawn Game

Just in time

The American Association adopted many National League rules, but it differed in three important ways. The clubs played on Sundays and holidays. The sale of beer was permitted in the ball parks, and admission was 25 cents, only half as much as the National League price.

The National League had nothing but contempt for the American Association. It sneered openly at every move made by the new league.

Soon the two leagues opened an all-out battle for talent. The American Association, with the backing of wealthy beer brewers, caused scores of good players to break their National League contracts. The National League owners quickly raised their salaries and lured players back. Some of the cases of contract-breaking landed in court, with one league suing the other.

In spite of the bickering, the American Association flourished. Fans liked Sunday ball, the low admission price, and the serving of beer at the ball parks. They also saw good baseball.

The Cincinnati Reds won the first pennant in the new league in 1882 and promptly arranged a series of games with the championship White Stockings of the National League. This might have turned into the first "World Series," but after each team won one game, the remainder of the games were called off. Angry league officials were opposed to any mingling of American Association and National League teams.

Then William Hulbert died unexpectedly, and A. H. Soden finished his term as National League president. The next year Colonel A. G. Mills, a man of great skill and patience, became president. Mills saw that the raiding between the two leagues could not go on. So he maneuvered leaders of both groups to a peace meeting, along with representatives of the Northwestern League, a minor circuit.

By the time the meeting was over, all three organizations had reached agreement on how future baseball business would be conducted. Essentially, the three leagues vowed to respect each other's territorial and player rights and, especially, the reserve list.

For a few years all went well. Baseball prospered. An attempt to start another major league in 1884 ended in failure. But the National League and the American Association continued to thrive. Realizing that they had to work together, they worked out a rule to control the sale of players from teams of one league to teams in the other. For example, if an American Association team wanted to sell a player to a National League team, it could do so only if all other teams in the Association approved. This is now known as the "waiver" rule.

Changes on the diamond helped baseball, too. Most of the changes concerned the rules that applied to pitcher and batter. The number of bad pitches that sent a batter to first base was gradually reduced from nine to four. The pitcher was also permitted, for the first time, to throw with any motion. The batter, however, still had the right to call for a high, or low, pitch.

10. Charles Comiskey

One new development above all others gave baseball a big boost. That was the practice of arranging games between league winners after the close of the season. Started by the Providence Grays and the New York Metropolitans in 1884, the post-season games met with immediate success.

A great new name—Charles A. Comiskey—was linked to the next four championship games. Comiskey, the Chicago-born son of a hard-working builder, was exposed to baseball at an early age. As a boy, he constantly irritated his father because of his interest in the game.

"Baseball is just a lot of tomfoolery," his father would complain. "To make a living, a man has to work, not play a game!"

Although Charles had great respect for his father, he couldn't overcome the lure of the diamond. He played with any amateur team that would take him. When his father sent him to college, he played on the college nine.

Soon after college, young Comiskey signed a contract with the Dubuque (Iowa) Rabbits for a small salary. Not long afterward, the tall, lean youngster won a first-base job with the St. Louis Browns. Then he became playing manager of the Browns.

Young Comiskey was both intelligent and hard-working. As manager of the Browns, he brought much to baseball. He introduced a big change in the way the infielders worked together on defense. First basemen, for instance, had always played close enough to the base to touch it. This meant that the second baseman had to try to field almost every ground ball batted between first and second.

Comiskey dropped the first-base position back and away from the base. In this way, the distance between first and second was covered by two players instead of one. As part of this change, Comiskey also taught his pitchers to run and cover first base whenever the first baseman fielded a grounder and could not make the put-out alone.

Comiskey tightened team defense even more by having infielders back up throws to the bases. If an outfield throw got past the third baseman, for example, another player was there to stop it and keep the runner from advancing.

This kind of baseball was apparently quite effective. The Browns, under Comiskey, won four pennants in a row, starting in 1885. Their first post-season opponent was the Chicago White Stockings with Adrian Anson as manager. The Chicago club was every bit as powerful as the Browns. The two teams met in both the second and third championship series. And what titanic struggles they were! The first time the teams played each other, the Browns won three, tied one, and lost three—one on a forfeit. The forfeit came about in the second game, when Comiskey took his team off the field after an umpire made a call he didn't like. The Browns claimed that the forfeited game didn't count and that they were the winners of the series.

The next year the Browns defeated the White Stockings in a six-game series. In 1887, however, they lost to Detroit in a fifteen-game match. The following season, 1888, they lost to New York in a ten-game series.

With the improvement in diamond play and league relationships, interest in baseball was at an all-time high. But unfortunately the owners and players were not getting along with each other.

11. The Battle Lines Are Drawn

The black list, the reserve list, and the new agreement among the professional leagues gave the baseball owners and officials tremendous power over the players.

The first abuse of this power occurred in 1885, when the leagues voted to limit players' salaries to $2,000. The clubs were also forbidden to give the players any advance salary during the winter. This worked a great hardship on players whenever they were faced with an emergency at home, or when they needed money to travel to meet the team at the start of the season.

The owners made matters worse by imposing fines and suspensions (without pay) for minor violations of the rules. One owner went so far as to fine a player for not tipping his hat when they passed on the street. Such treatment made the players bitter and angry. They talked of joining together to fight the owners.

The first move in that direction took place in the fall of 1885. The New York Giants formed a chapter of a new organization called The Brotherhood of Professional Base Ball Players. President of the organization was handsome, popular John Montgomery Ward, the Giants' pitcher and shortstop. Once the New York players were organized, Ward began to form chapters among other clubs. As the Brotherhood grew, the players began to make known their position on various issues. They asked that full salaries be written into their contracts. And they demanded that an end be put both to the rule limiting salaries and to the hated reserve list. By the end of the season, the Brotherhood had almost 100 members enrolled. They felt it was time to discuss matters with the owners and demand recognition for themselves.

At Al Spalding's suggestion, the National League agreed to talk with the Brotherhood representatives. The owners, however, played a shrewd game. They were very polite and agreed to a few minor changes in player rules. Then they pointed out that, after all, the players were already signed for the following year. Furthermore, the American Association was not represented.

How could they make any further changes?

28

John Ward may have seen through these tactics, but he probably felt the Brotherhood was not strong enough to risk an open fight. In any event, he agreed it would be useless to press matters further.

The playing season of 1888 followed its usual course. And after it ended, the hard-fisted owners forgot many of their previous promises to the Brotherhood.

At first this deceit didn't seem to matter. Most of the players were excited about something else. They had heard that Al Spalding was taking two teams to New Zealand and Australia. The prospect of a long ocean voyage to strange lands struck the fancy of American baseball players and fans. In fact it seemed almost unbelievable at a time when a trip across one's home state was a rarity.

The talk about the trip turned out to be true. Spalding, one of the owners of the Chicago White Stockings and president of a sporting-goods firm, had succeeded in arranging such a tour.

One of the two teams to make the trip was the White Stockings, managed by Cap Anson. The other was the All-Americans, a group of what would now be called "all-stars." The All-Americans were picked by their manager, John Ward.

The tour was significant in many ways. The President of the United States gave the team a send-off at a White House reception. This was a new and high honor for baseball. Later, amidst much excitement, the party of 35 players and their wives started their long westward journey from Chicago. On the way to the Pacific Coast, the teams

John M. Ward, Capt. New York B. B. Club.   586

Newsboy   NEW YORK.

played in Denver, Omaha, and other cities. Few people west of Chicago had ever seen big-league baseball. Wherever the teams played, they were watched by great crowds of people, many of whom had traveled miles.

In Sydney, Australia, the All-Americans and the White Stockings played before 5,500 spectators. In Melbourne the crowd numbered 11,000. By the time the Australian trip was finished, the players had been invited to extend their tour to Africa, Asia, and Europe. They went next to Ceylon, then to Egypt, where they actually played a ball game on the desert sands near the ancient pyramids.

From Egypt the Americans traveled to Rome, where games were played on royal grounds before the King of Italy and his court. Leaving Rome, the group went on to Florence, then northward to France and England.

While John Ward, the president of the Brotherhood, was off on this expedition, the team owners were busily fashioning a new noose to slip around the necks of their ball players. Originated by John T. Brush, owner of the Indianapolis team, it was called the Classification Plan. Under the plan, the best players were classified as "A" players. They were to receive $2,500 a year and no more. The next best player was put in the "B" classification and was to receive $2,250. The new pay scale went all the way down to $1,500 for Class "E" players.

The owners claimed to have rated each player on conduct and effort. The plan shocked the players, but the owners said they would be blackballed if they didn't agree to the plan. With Ward away and no one else willing to lead the Brotherhood, the situation seemed hopeless to the players. Most of them reluctantly signed contracts. Thus the owners succeeded in putting the Classification Plan into effect. They were soon to regret it.

12. The Revolt

The steamer *Adriatic*, bearing the touring American baseball teams, was sighted off Long Island on April 6, 1889. She was three days late. Her tardiness, however, had not discouraged those awaiting her arrival. Some had important news to convey to John Ward. Others were anxious to speak with Al Spalding.

Two boats were already racing to meet the *Adriatic* in the farther reaches of Lower New York Bay. One was the steamer *Laura M. Storin*, "loaded with lovers of baseball," as one newspaper put it. The other was a tugboat, carrying a score of prominent actors and actresses, presumably lovers of the game.

When the three vessels came together, a great cheer went up amid a shriek of foghorns and whistles and the clanging of ship's bells.

In Egypt, Spalding's American baseball party posed under the broken nose of the Sphinx.

Very quickly a gangplank was run out to bridge the gap between the *Adriatic* and the *Laura M. Storin.* The ball players and their wives piled aboard the little steamer, which quickly made her way back to the island of Manhattan.

Not until the party was on its way to breakfast at the Fifth Avenue Hotel did John Ward learn how the Brotherhood had been betrayed by the new Classification Plan. When he tried to protest to Al Spalding a few days later, Ward was told there was nothing to discuss.

Spalding's blunt dismissal was too much even for patient John Ward. That summer the players began to meet secretly. Their plan? A new league. A committee was formed to raise funds. They had no difficulty, for Ward and his friends knew a number of men with money to invest who were sympathetic to baseball. As soon as these men were approached, however, word of the Brotherhood plans leaked out.

Spalding was one of the first to hear. He tried to arrange a meeting with Ward. But Ward said simply:

"Remember, Al, there's nothing to discuss."

By the fall of 1889, the players and their new owners formed a partnership to operate the "Players' League." John Ward called the press to a downtown Manhattan hotel early in November to make the official announcement. Along with the plans for the new league, Ward issued a blistering "manifesto."

". . . There was a time," it went, "when the League stood for integrity and fair dealing. Today it stands for dollars and cents. Once it looked to the elevation of the game and an honest exhibition of the sport. Today its eyes are upon the turnstiles. Men have come into the business for no other motive than to exploit it for every dollar in sight. Measures originally intended for the good of the game have been turned into instruments for wrong. . . . Players have been bought and sold and exchanged as though they were sheep instead of American citizens. . . ."

The launching of the Players' League in 1890 started another all-out baseball war. With rules that abolished the abuses and included profit-sharing, the League drew almost every big-name player in the major leagues. About the only big star of the day who did not join was stubborn Cap Anson.

The American Association and the National League, united and experienced, fought the Players' League in every way imaginable. They scheduled games wherever and whenever the Players' games were scheduled. They pooled their money to carry the weaker teams. They changed their contracts and offered bonuses and bigger contracts to members of the Players' League if they would leave the new league.

In a typical attempt to break the Brotherhood, Spalding had a secret meeting with Michael Kelly who, at that time, was at the peak of his ability.

After a preliminary discussion, Spalding laid a check in front of Kelly.

"As you will notice, that check is good for $10,000 and payable to you," Spalding said to the king. "That's yours for signing with our league. On top of that, you can have a three-year contract."

"For how much?" Kelly countered.

"You can fill in the amount of salary yourself."

Kelly looked Spalding squarely in the eye. Convinced that Spalding meant what he said, Kelly replied:

"I'll take a walk and think it over. Meet you here in half an hour."

Kelly's walk lasted about two hours.

"Al," he said on his return, "I just can't do it. I can't go back on the Brotherhood—all my friends."

Kelly paused for a moment, then added: "And neither would you, Al."

"I understand," Spalding said. "And you're right—I wouldn't either."

The fans, however, became discouraged and disgusted with all the scrapping. Because their favorite players were continually moving from one team to another, they found it hard to get into a rooting frame of mind. Then too it was hard to decide which game to attend if two or three teams were playing in the same city on the same day. As a result the fans stayed away from the ball parks. And all three leagues lost a tremendous amount of money.

At first it was hard to tell just who was winning the battle. All the teams gave out false attendance figures. Then came one seemingly sure indication. Cincinnati of the American Association, unable to keep afloat financially, sold out to the Players'. This was a bitter blow to the opponents of the Players' League. By the end of the season, almost everybody seemed to be in the mood for a compromise. Even the backers of the Players' League—as distinct from the Brotherhood—were looking for a way out of the unhappy war.

There were many secret meetings, and out of these grew three committees—one representing each league. Al Spalding was head of the National League committee. Smart as a fox when it came to business, Spalding found a way to break the Players' League. He did it by insisting that he could meet only with the financial backers of the Players' League. Ward and the other members of the Brotherhood, he said, did not have control of the money, so how could they speak for the owners?

Ward fought hard to maintain a united stand. But he could not overcome Spalding's "divide and conquer" methods. One by one, the backers of the Players' League teams sold out.

By winter there was no more Players' League. In its place was a new line-up of major league teams, covered by a new set of rules.

With the Players' League dead and a costly war ended, all should have been peaceful and serene in the world of baseball. But it wasn't; there were other arguments. Before the 1891 season opened, baseball was in its fourth war in 15 years! The pattern was the same as in all the war years. Rival leagues were plotting against each other for players.

By the end of 1891, the major leagues were again looking for peace. And they had the usual reason—losses at the gate.

To end all their troubles, they agreed to a grand new plan. The strongest teams in both leagues would be merged into one—The National League and the American Association of Professional

33

Base Ball Clubs. (Actually only four Association teams—Baltimore, Washington, St. Louis, and Louisville—joined the eight existing National League teams to form the big new organization.)

With one unified 12-team league, it seemed as if there would be little opportunity for any more fighting.

13. From Infancy to Adolescence

With the start of the first 12-team major league, a change came over baseball. New and younger players began to appear. The playing rules came closer to perfection. And the term "inside baseball" came into use.

Harry Wright had introduced the first noticeable team play. Spalding, Anson, then Comiskey, helped develop it. But Frank Selee, the manager of the Boston National League team, was the one who made so much of it that the fans took notice. Selee, for example, favored the hit-and-run play, which has thrilled fans for years. Selee's method was a little different from the one in use today, but the principle is the same.

When you look at a baseball team in the field, you will notice that the first and second basemen space themselves so they can cover most of the area between first and second base. The third baseman and shortstop share the area between second and third. If any of these players pull out of position, a large hole is left in the defense.

Frank Selee found a way to *make* the defensive players move. When he had a runner on first, he would signal for the hit-and-run play. As the pitcher got ready to throw to the batter, the runner on first base would break for second. Either the shortstop or second baseman, or both, would have to rush to cover second. They had to guard against a steal of second. The batter, of course, would then try to knock the ball through the hole in the defense. If he was successful, the runner could get one or two extra bases. An extra base was very important in the era of the dead ball.

Selee's teams won three pennants in a row, starting in 1891. The Boston fans were delighted with the power and speed of Selee's team. But interest in the remaining 11 cities lagged. It was obvious that the fans preferred the excitement of two pennant races in smaller and better balanced leagues. They liked the after-season climax, too. This was missing in the 12-team circuit.

In an attempt to spark more interest, the league went to a "split season" in 1892. They established for the first time a 154-game schedule and decided that the winner of the first half would play the winner of the second half for the championship.

Boston won the top spot in its half of the league. And a new name among ball players led Cleveland to victory in the other half of the league. The team was the Cleveland Spiders. The new player —Denton True Young.

Young was an industrious farm boy who stood six feet two in his spikes and tipped the scale at 210 pounds. An ability to throw a tremendous fast ball gave Young a nickname that made fans forget his first and second names. As he was warming up one day in front of an old wooden backstop, his catcher let two or three pitches go by. Each time that happened, the ball whizzed into the backstop, breaking a board.

"Boy, looks like a cyclone hit it," commented Young's manager as he inspected the damage. From then on, the rawboned youngster was known as "Cyclone," or "Cy" Young.

Young made an auspicious start when he broke into baseball. He struck out Cap Anson the first time he faced the fearsome Chicago hitter. Young also ended his career spectacularly. In 22 seasons, he amassed 510 victories, a record number of games too—906.

When Boston and Cleveland met in the first game of their play-off series, the game ended in an 11-inning scoreless tie that was called off because of darkness. Boston won the remaining games, however.

While 1893 was the year Boston won its third straight pennant, it was also the year the pitching rules underwent their last major change. The pitching distance went to 60 feet 6 inches, which is what it is today at almost all levels of baseball played by those 13 and older.

Other rules, too, had become more

Because of the way he pitched, Denton True Young earned the nickname of "Cy"—short for cyclone.

stabilized. The number of bad pitches that entitled a batter to a base had gradually changed from nine, to eight, to seven, to five, and finally, to four. At the start of the 1883 season, the pitcher was permitted to throw the ball from any spot beneath his shoulder. But all restrictions were lifted the next year.

For a long time the batter had been able to tell the pitcher where he wanted the ball thrown. If the pitcher failed to comply, the batter was awarded first base. On the other hand, the umpire couldn't call a strike unless the pitch was in a zone indicated by the batter. By 1888, this was eliminated and the traditional "three strikes and out!" call was started.

With that change, baseball moved into one of its most exciting eras.

14. The Original Orioles

Under Ned Hanlon, the Baltimore Orioles of 1894 became the greatest team in baseball. They were greater even than the past teams of the Cincinnati Red Stockings, Chicago White Stockings, and the Boston machines built by Frank Selee.

The Orioles boasted only one star, Wee Willie Keeler. But they didn't need to be great individually, for they played as no other nine had done up to that time. They played as a *team*.

One of the Oriole players of that day was a scrawny, runty third baseman with oversized ears. His name was John McGraw. He didn't look big enough to make the average high school team. But what he lacked in size, McGraw made up for in skill, courage, and sheer ferocity.

A native of upstate New York, McGraw was the son of poor parents. His love for baseball drove his father to distraction. He lived and breathed the game from the day he was strong enough to pick up a bat and ball to the day he died.

Townspeople shook their heads in wonder as they watched McGraw grow up. He practiced throwing and hitting at every opportunity. When he became old enough to work, he worked only to earn money for buying baseball equipment. He was especially fond of rule books, buying every new one published.

McGraw first played professional baseball in the New York-Pennsylvania League in 1890. He was still a youngster. The following year he joined several other players and signed to play for a Florida team for "board, shaving and washing expenses and a cigar a week." His smart heads-up play, deft glove, accurate throwing arm, and consistent batting soon got him into the majors.

Another talented Oriole player was

catcher Wilbert Robinson. A good-natured hulk of a man, Robinson was easily one of the smartest players in baseball.

The Orioles were a brash, swashbuckling crew who liked, above all else, to win ball games. And by any means. Some of their efforts were scientific; some were a clear evasion of the rules. As an example of the former, the Orioles used the hit-and-run play to perfection. Against the Giants in the opening game in 1894, for example, they used it 13 times successfully. They also developed something new: the "squeeze" play. Just as today, a runner on third base broke for the plate as the pitcher delivered the ball. The batter bunted the ball, enabling the runner to score.

As an example of their not-so-scientific methods, the Oriole outfield often planted extra baseballs in the high outfield grass before play started. If a sharp liner bounded by the outfielders, the nearest player didn't have to chase the ball until it stopped rolling. All the outfielder had to do was pick up one of the planted balls and hurl it into play.

This plan backfired one day as two outfielders ran after a ball driven between them. One Oriole picked up a hidden ball, whirled, and threw to the infield. At the same time the other Oriole tossed in the batted ball. The umpire was quick to catch on. He forfeited the game to the Orioles' opponent!

McGraw and his mates not only used the hidden-ball trick, they also blocked the base paths and held on to runners whenever they could do so without get-

John McGraw, the runty Oriole third baseman with oversized ears.

ting caught. One of McGraw's favorite tricks was to grab a runner by the belt when he tried to break for the plate after the catch of a fly ball by the outfield. This, too, went amiss one day. His opponent knew the trick and unbuckled his belt when McGraw wasn't looking. The fly ball plopped into an Oriole outfielder's glove and the runner lit out for home. McGraw, dumbfounded, was left with a belt dangling from his hand.

In 1894 the Orioles swept to their very first pennant. And they repeated their success the next two years. The original Orioles left an unmistakable mark on baseball. And through the many Oriole players who later became managers—McGraw, Robinson, and Hugh Jennings—the spirit of that famous team was carried to others.

15. Fandom Balks

In spite of the many improvements in baseball during the 1890s, the conduct of the game dipped to a new low. The owners were foolish in the way they ran their top-heavy league. Though they had the monopoly they had always wanted, they were so greedy and selfish they almost wrecked their business.

To begin with, the owners were dishonest with each other. For example, it was the practice for visiting teams and home teams to share the gate proceeds on a percentage basis (usually 60% for the home team, 40% for the visitors). In a number of instances, the home team falsely reported gate receipts. This meant the visiting team failed to get its fair share.

The deals involving sales and trades of players were often crooked, too. The owners were as ruthless with the players as they had been before the Brotherhood revolt. When the National League and the American Association merged, it was agreed that all players who signed contracts before December, 1891, were to go back to the clubs holding these contracts. All other players' names were thrown into a pool. From this pool the teams picked enough men to fill a 15-man roster. The leftover players were sent to the minor leagues.

The following year, to hold down expenses, the owners cut two men from each team. They then arbitrarily reduced salaries—some by as much as 40%! The owners abused their rigid control over the players in other ways. They fined them at the slightest whim, held back salaries, and refused to pay legitimate expenses.

The owners apparently didn't care about the interests and loyalties of the fans either. Many invested in more than one team. This made the fans wonder if teams were competing on a fair basis. John T. Brush, for example, owned stock in both Cincinnati and the New York

Giants. And in 1899 the owner of the Cleveland Spiders also owned the St. Louis entry. Because St. Louis seemed a more profitable location than Cleveland, this owner moved his best players to St. Louis. To the disgust and indignation of the Cleveland fans, the Spiders finished with the worst record in baseball. They lost 134 games and won but 20!

On top of all this, the owners paid little attention to what was going on between the foul lines. The diamond often appeared to be more of a place for a gang fight than for a ball game. Because the players were out to win by fair means or foul—and more often foul than fair—brawling and fighting became common. The umpires had no authority.

The League paid them a small sum to run ball games, then forgot about them.

For a while one umpire handled the games. A two-umpire system was started in 1895, but matters didn't improve. The poor umpires were stomped on, pushed, and generally abused. The owners were too busy listening to the click of the turnstiles to take notice.

As baseball moved through the 1890s, some of its worst features came to the fore. Competition was tainted, and teams were often out of control. And the owners, in their greediness, ignored the public. This short-sighted handling of America's newest and biggest entertainment business was to have unfortunate results which the owners would soon regret.

16. A New League, a New Attitude

There was unrest in many quarters over the policies of the National League, especially when the League slowly began to fall apart.

One of those who had new ideas about baseball was Charles Comiskey. While managing the Cincinnati Reds, Comiskey met a big, dynamic sports writer for the Cincinnati *Commercial-Gazette*. His name was Bancroft Johnson. Soon they became fast friends. Like all good friends they had a common interest. Theirs was baseball, but not the kind of baseball then in style. Comiskey and Johnson wanted clean baseball—baseball

for the fans.

In 1894, at Comiskey's suggestion, a number of teams formed a minor league in the north-central area of the country. Called the Western League, it included such cities as Minneapolis, Milwaukee, Toledo, Kansas City, Detroit, Sioux City, Grand Rapids, and Indianapolis. Comiskey attended the first meeting of the new organization and agreed to take the franchise at St. Paul. He nominated Ban Johnson for president of the League, and Johnson was promptly accepted.

During this fateful meeting, the Milwaukee franchise was given to a man

Cornelius McGillicuddy, better known to baseball fans as Connie Mack.

Charles A. Comiskey

named Cornelius McGillicuddy, a tall, skinny ex-catcher who became known to later generations as Connie Mack. Mack, like Comiskey, had played and managed in the Players' League. Mack was happy to be in the Western League. Like Comiskey and Johnson, he was opposed to drinking, gambling, and rowdyism.

As a young catcher, Mack had been one of the first to try to distract opposing hitters by chattering away at them as they stood at the plate. But he was always polite. Once he even apologized for tipping an opponent's bat.

As Mack, Comiskey, and Johnson worked to build up the Western League, they looked ahead to the time when they could bring it into competition with the National League. The baseball monopoly that existed in the 1890s was very strong, however. Those who wished to oppose it—and there were many—had to move carefully.

In 1899 Ban Johnson announced that the Western Association was reorganizing and would take the field in 1900 as the American League.

While this was going on, the National League was having internal trouble. As the teams lost money, the owners drifted into two warring camps. One side backed Andrew Freedman, an owner of the New York Giants. The other side opposed him.

As one way of getting out of their difficulties, the National League dropped four teams for 1900. Ban Johnson quickly moved an American franchise into one of the cities, Cleveland. He also put Comiskey in Chicago with another American League franchise. These two moves angered the National League, even though Johnson clearly indicated he was not interested in starting another baseball war.

With the launching of the American League, Johnson put a new face on baseball. His methods were simple. He took a strong stand with the players. He appointed a good corps of umpires, treated them fairly, and backed their every decision. The American League games were run in an orderly manner. Rowdyism, drinking, gambling, and profanity were prohibited. Those who didn't abide by Johnson's rules were fined and suspended.

The fans were weary of the type of baseball being played in the National League. They were also suspicious of the shadowy operations of the owners. Right from the start, they supported the infant American League, enabling it to become a fairly prosperous organization.

By the end of that first year, however, the American League had learned that it was useless to try to exist peacefully with the haughty National Leaguers.

"If they want a war, that's what they'll get," was the attitude Johnson adopted.

His next big step was to establish the American League as a second major league by putting teams in several big eastern cities where they competed directly with National League teams. McGraw, who had also become dissatisfied with the National League, was given an American League franchise in Baltimore. Connie Mack—without a ball park, with few funds, but with more than enough confidence and courage—moved into Philadelphia. Hugh Duffy replaced him at Milwaukee. The American League also put teams in Boston and Washington. Before long many of the prominent National League players were jumping to the Johnson circuit.

17. A Close Call

The National League continued to be in bad shape during the first two years of the new century. The internal fighting, the battle with the American League, and a big drop in attendance all added to its troubles. The owners were in a desperate mood.

During the summer of 1901 Andrew Freedman and three others hatched an incredible plan to solve their difficulties. Freedman was a stubborn, ruthless man

with a special talent for making enemies. As owner of the controlling interest in the New York Giants, he had defied the National League, the players, the fans—anyone who opposed him.

Freedman's answer to the problems of the National League was to turn the organization into a trust. This corporation or syndicate could control every aspect of the game. There would be one owner instead of eight. Franchises and

41

players could easily be shifted wherever and whenever it would do the corporation the most good. Competition among the teams, of course, would become a farce. But Freedman and his friends didn't care about that. They were interested only in making a profit.

A sports writer somehow learned of the plot and printed the whole story. Once the news was out, the four owners who had not conspired with Freedman demanded a showdown.

It came during the League's winter meetings in New York. Barney Dreyfuss, owner of the Pirates, insisted that the League elect a new president.

"I nominate Al Spalding," he said.

This startled the Freedman group, since Spalding was in retirement.

They recovered quickly, however, and cast four votes against Spalding. The other four voted for Spalding.

Spalding's name was put to a vote again. The results were the same. Four votes for Spalding, four against.

There was a great deal of argument as the voting went on. Finally the meeting broke up, and both sides vowed to settle the matter the next day.

As the eight owners and Nick Young, the National League president, gathered together in the meeting room to resume the voting, the door opened quietly. To the amazement of the Freedman group, in walked Al Spalding.

"Good morning, gentlemen," Spalding said. "I've come to talk to you about the future of baseball." Spalding, an eloquent and forceful speaker, proceeded to appeal to the owners not to syndicate baseball.

Albert G. Spalding

"Such a move would mean the ruination of the game," he said.

When he was finished, Spalding left as quickly and quietly as he had entered. He then called a press conference. First he produced documents that confirmed the plot to turn the League into a syndicate. The syndicate, according to the plans, was to be run by a board of five managers, headed by a president.

In strong and plain language, Spalding made his views clear. There must be no syndication of baseball, he insisted, because such a system would mean that ". . . one man or half a dozen men might dominate the entire business —and with villainous brutality. . . ." Then Spalding went on to say that Freedman, if elected president, would have to quit baseball "because . . . on his baseball record, I say Freedman is more kinds of a fool than ever before existed in baseball."

It was a clever move on Spalding's part, for it brought great press and public pressure to bear on the Freedman forces. But still the matter of a new president of the National League had to be resolved.

The balloting resumed. This time Nick Young was nominated for reëlection. Time after time, however, the balloting results were the same: four votes for Spalding, four votes for Young.

Finally Freedman and his supporters became exhausted. They made a motion to adjourn the meeting. The motion went to a vote. The results? Four to four!

Completely out of patience, Freedman and his friends left the meeting room, empowering Young to vote for them. Soon, however, Young could stay awake no longer.

"The meeting is adjourned," he said. Since there was no quorum, he was sure no business could be transacted in his absence.

He was wrong.

John Rogers, owner of the Philadelphia club, was voted to the chair. Then a strange thing happened. A man named Knowles, who was Freedman's secretary, put his head in the meeting-room door. He apparently wanted to see what was going on and report back to his boss.

John Rogers quickly announced:

"With F. M. Knowles of the New York Giants present, we now have a quorum. Proceed with the voting for president."

Although Knowles quickly withdrew, Al Spalding was elected president of the National League on the twenty-sixth ballot by a vote of 4 to 0.

By that time it was after 1:00 A.M. on a Saturday morning. Rogers and his three companions awakened Spalding and told him the news.

"All right boys," Spalding said. "If that's the way you want it I'll go along. One thing, though—we must get possession of the League records. I saw them in a large trunk under a table in the meeting room."

At 4:00 A.M., Spalding roused Nick Young, told him he was the new president, and demanded the League records. Young refused. While the two men argued, two hotel porters slipped into the meeting room, picked up the trunk, and carried it to Spalding's quarters.

The next day Spalding called another press conference. He told an excited group of sports writers he was the newly elected president of the National League and outlined some broad plans for improvement of the League. In closing, Spalding commented that he assumed his election meant that Freedman was out of baseball.

Freedman, hot with anger at the turn of events, was not quite out of baseball, however. He secured a court injunction to prevent Spalding from taking office.

Spalding was too fast. He got out of the state before the papers could be served. Finally the Freedman faction knew it was licked. Freedman gave up his interest in the Giants. As soon as that happened, Spalding resigned.

Baseball had, indeed, been saved.

43

18. Peace! It's Wonderful!

Shortly after the start of the new century, baseball began to enjoy a prosperity it had never known before. There were several reasons for this. First, the leagues had finally become stable, and they were working together. At the annual meetings of 1902 and 1903, the National and American leagues buried the hatchet. A new agreement was drawn up to cover both the major and minor leagues. It also established the important player and territorial rights so essential to the orderly conduct of the game. By the end of 1902 the American League was located in Chicago, Cleveland, St. Louis, New York, Detroit, Boston, Washington, and Philadelphia. There were no more changes for half a century.

The rule makers had also finally found the proper balance between offense and defense. And, perhaps most important of all, a host of exciting new names and personalities appeared. Combined, these factors produced thrilling pennant races. They also built up intercity rivalries and won back the confidence of the public.

Among the "greats" of the era was a big, raw-boned rookie named John Peter Wagner, who came to be known as "Hans," then "Honus." Wagner broke into professional baseball in 1895 in the Michigan State League. He moved to Paterson of the Atlantic League for the next two years, then made the jump to the major leagues, signing with Louisville. In 1900, however, the Louisville Club was owned by the same man who held the Pittsburgh franchise. The Louisville team was broken up, and its best players were moved to Pittsburgh. Among them was Wagner.

Wagner looked like anything but a ball player. He was square of build and slightly bow-legged. A huge pair of hands dangled from long, powerful arms. When he moved, he looked like a big bear.

But Wagner, like King Kelly before him, could do anything on the diamond. During the early part of his career, he played every position. He pitched, caught, played the outfield and infield. In 1902, however, Pittsburgh's playing manager, Fred Clarke, stationed Wagner at shortstop. And there he stayed until 1917, playing 2,785 games, a League record.

With Wagner and Clarke starring in the field and at bat, the Pittsburgh Pirates won three straight pennants, beginning with 1901.

In 1904, Christy Mathewson, another all-time great, burst upon the baseball world. In the course of his 16-year period in the majors, Mathewson won 373 games. Many say he was the game's best pitcher.

Mathewson started in professional ball in 1899, with a salary of $90 a month. After a year in the New England League, he moved to Norfolk. He had a trial with the Giants, but lost his first three games and was sent back to Norfolk by Andrew Freedman. Mathewson was not disturbed by his showing with

Honus Wagner (below), the raw-boned Pittsburgh shortstop who could do almost anything on the diamond.

Both pitcher Christy Mathewson (upper right) and catcher Roger Bresnahan (left) won fame as Giant stars.

45

the Giants. He went on to win 21 games at Norfolk, while losing but two. He was drafted by Cincinnati, then traded back to the Giants.

Mathewson started off with a bang. The second time he put on his Giant uniform, he won eight in a row, four by shut-outs. In his ninth appearance, he lost 1-0. By the end of the season, he had appeared in 40 games, pitching more than 300 innings. He had 20 victories to his credit, including one no-hit game.

In 1902 Mathewson became one of the first pitchers of the new era to win 30 games. In each of the following two years he won the same number.

Another Giant pitcher who made history in the early 1900s was Joe McGinnity. In 1903 he pitched in 55 games, winning 31 and losing 19. Three times during August, McGinnity pitched both games in double-headers. And he won them all!

The Giant's catcher, Roger Bresnahan, was another remarkable performer of the period. Few catchers in all the history of the game can compare with Bresnahan. He was a tough fighter, exceptionally fast on the base paths, and a powerful hitter. He also satisfied Giant manager John McGraw, the old Oriole star, with the way he ran the defense—something few players could do. (Bresnahan is credited with being the first catcher to wear shin guards.)

One of the most remarkable pitchers of that day was George Edward Waddell, a six-foot, three-inch giant. Waddell, called "Rube" by everyone, was an utter child. At the slightest provocation

"Rube" Waddell, Connie Mack's remarkable but unreliable pitcher.

he would wander off the field. Once, just as he was to take the mound, a fire engine went clanging by the ball park. Waddell immediately took off after it.

Waddell was eccentric and unreliable, for sure. But, oh, how he could pitch! He had to wander about the minor leagues for a long time, however, before a major-league manager would take a chance on him. The first and only manager who could handle the childish

46

pitcher was Connie Mack. And even Mack didn't have an easy time of it.

Mack first heard of Waddell while managing the Milwaukee team. Needing another strong pitcher, he sent for the big-shouldered Rube, who was playing semi-professional ball in Pennsylvania. For almost two weeks Mack sent a daily telegram to Rube, offering him a job with Milwaukee. Finally the pitcher responded by a telegram.

"Come and get me," it said.

Mack did just that. To get Waddell out of town, however, he had to pay some of the pitcher's debts and rescue his belongings from a hock shop.

Some of Waddell's most memorable games were against the redoubtable Cy Young. On May 5, 1904, Young beat Waddell by hurling a perfect game. The next year Waddell beat Young in a 3–2 thriller that went to 20 innings.

Mack often said that Waddell—with a burning fast ball and a big curve that traveled at about the same speed—had more natural throwing ability than any pitcher he had ever seen. He was probably right.

Mack was blessed with other fine pitchers in the 1900s. One of them was Edward Stewart Plank, a left-hander. Mack found Plank on the campus of Gettysburg College. Plank was one of the few lefties to win 300 or more games.

Mordecai Peter Centennial Brown of the Chicago Cubs was still another pitcher who drew nation-wide attention. While working on a farm during his youth, Brown had lost the index finger of his throwing hand. The finger next to it was also badly maimed. As a result, he was known as "Three Finger" Brown.

In the midst of one of baseball's bitterest rivalries, Brown and the great Christy Mathewson had a remarkable series of pitching duels. In June of 1905, for instance, Brown and Mathewson matched each other pitch for pitch throughout nine innings. Neither side got a hit or a run. Finally Brown weakened and surrendered two hits. The Giants won 1-0.

Following that defeat, however, the Chicago Cubs, with Brown on the mound, beat Mathewson nine straight. Brown and Mathewson pitched against each other 24 times over a 13-year period with Brown winning 13 of the games.

19. The One-Run Days

The baseball used in the first decade of this century had less bounce per foot than any employed before or since. Hitters couldn't drive the ball very far, and one run was often the difference between victory and defeat.

The old-timers say the dead-ball days were the best because the team at bat had to vary its attack in order to get a run. The players had to steal, bunt, and use the hit-and-run and squeeze plays much more often than today. The oldsters also point out that, in today's game, one blow by the weakest hitter on the team can bring a pitcher's battle to a quick end.

Other fans are opposed to the one-run game because it gives the pitcher too powerful a role in the contest.

Whatever the answer may be, baseball was obviously a mighty thrilling spectacle between 1900 and 1910. And that is just about how long the dead ball lasted.

In 1904, for example, the New York Highlanders were in a neck-and-neck battle with the Boston Red Sox. On the last day of the season, the teams met in a double-header at the Polo Grounds. A split of the games would mean a tie. To win the pennant, the Highlanders needed to take both.

With Jack Chesbro on the mound for the first game, the Highlanders' chances looked promising.

But Chesbro had his hands full. When he strode from the dugout to start the ninth inning, the score was tied at 2–2. Red Sox catcher Lou Criger opened with a single. A sacrifice bunt put him on second base. An infield out moved him to third.

Chesbro needed only one out to get out of the inning. His next pitch, however, bounded past the catcher and Criger scored what proved to be the winning run. For years fans said it was the costliest wild pitch ever unfurled by a moundsman.

The Red Sox fans, still tingling over their victory against the Highlanders, looked forward to a championship series with the New York Giants, managed by John McGraw. The Giants were the winners of the National League pennant. But Giant owner John Brush still carried a grudge against Ban Johnson and would have no part of such a championship game.

"The American League is still bush," was the attitude of Brush and his manager, John McGraw. "They're not in a class with the Giants."

Such disdainful treatment of the Red Sox and the American League in general aroused a storm of protest. All was smoothed over at the winter meetings, however. Both leagues decided it would be profitable and wise to arrange an annual series between the winners of each league. And that's how the World Series—inaugurated in 1905—was officially established.

A fiction writer couldn't have made the first modern World Series more dramatic. McGraw's Giants, with Mathew-

The New York Highlanders—later to become the Yankees—play the Philadelphia Athletics at the Polo Grounds in 1907.

Frank Chance, first baseman and manager of the Chicago Cubs.

hanging out the train window on the return trip to Philadelphia. With Waddell on the sidelines, Mathewson dominated the series. Over a period of six days, Matty pitched three games against the Athletics. He won them all by shut-outs. During the 27 scoreless innings, Matty gave up 14 hits and struck out 18 Athletics, one of them five times. He walked but one man.

The Giants made McGraw look good by taking the Series four games to one.

The Giants didn't win the next year, though. Starting in 1906, the remarkable Chicago Cubs won the flag in four out of five campaigns.

The Cubs, along with Three Finger Brown, had a fine infield. Their double-play combination included shortstop

One of the all-time greats, Ty Cobb, demonstrates his famous batting grip.

son, McGinnity, and Bresnahan turning in one glittering performance after another, won the National pennant again.

In the American League, Connie Mack's strong mound corps of Waddell, Plank, and Bender gave the Athletics the flag. Although the fans looked forward to watching gentle Connie Mack match wits with the fiery McGraw, they wanted most of all to see what would happen when Waddell and Mathewson met.

Waddell never made the World Series that year. The Rube injured his shoulder—not on the ball diamond, but in a wrestling match at the Boston railroad station. Rube fell heavily on his pitching shoulder, then slept with his arm

Joe Tinker, second baseman John Evers and first baseman and manager Frank Chance. So many times did this trio thwart Giant rallies that the witty Franklin P. Adams wrote that the saddest possible words on the diamond were—

"Tinker to Evers to Chance."

While the Cubs roared through the National League to set a 1906 record of 116 victories, the Chicago White Sox won in the American League. Although dubbed the "hitless wonders" because they batted an anemic .228, the White Sox defeated the Cubs in World Series play by a score of 4 games to 2.

In moving toward the pennant, the White Sox had to squeeze past the Athletics and a new powerhouse—the Detroit Tigers. The Tiger lineup included an outfielder baseball fans would be hearing more about—Tyrus Raymond Cobb.

During his 24 years in the Big Leagues, the Tiger outfielder collected 4,191 base hits for a lifetime batting average of .367. No player who has been in major-league baseball for 10 years or more can come close to that record.

Cobb first won the American League batting title in 1907. He won it 11 more times, 9 in succession. On three occasions his average was over .400. Only one other modern player—Rogers Hornsby—equaled that record.

Cobb was the first player elected to baseball's Hall of Fame. Many consider him the greatest player of all time. It's hard to believe, but 16 of the many records set by Cobb still stand. Some of them, like his record of 829 stolen bases, may never be broken. Of course, records alone never give a full picture of a player or a team. This was particularly true in the case of Ty Cobb, one of baseball's most daring and fearless ball players.

20. The Merkle Incident

In their wildest dreams, ball fans could not have imagined what was in store for them during the 1908 season. In the American League three teams— the Cleveland Naps, the Detroit Tigers, and the Chicago White Sox—fought it out right down to the *last day* of the season. Then, by beating Chicago, Detroit nosed out Cleveland by a half a game.

Before that spectacular finish, however, White Sox pitcher Edward A. Walsh had put on an astounding show.

He appeared in 66 games, started 55, and finished all but six. At the close of the season, he had 40 victories to his credit, as against 15 losses.

That same season Ed Reulbach of the Chicago Cubs drew almost as much comment as Walsh. In the National League the Cubs were fighting a fierce three-cornered battle with the New York Giants and Pittsburgh Pirates. At one point in the contest, Reulbach hurled 44 scoreless innings, a feat that went un-

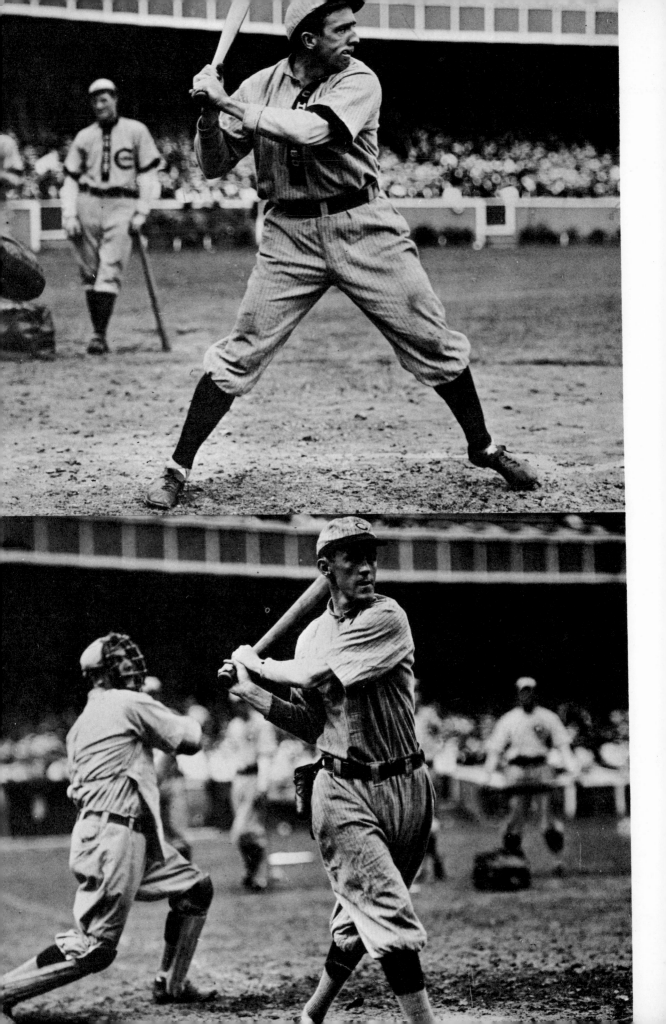

matched until 1933. In the midst of that string, he shut out Brooklyn in a double-header by scores of 5–0 and 3–0.

Reulbach's toil might have gone for naught, however, had it not been for the heads-up play of teammate Johnny Evers. The Chicago second baseman, alert and persistent, touched off an incident that will live in baseball history books forever.

To appreciate what happened, one must go back to September 4 of that memorable season and review one play that took place in a game between the Cubs and Pirates at Pittsburgh.

It was the bottom of the tenth inning. Neither the Pirates nor the Cubs had scored. But Pirate manager Fred Clarke was on third base, with Warren Gill on first. At bat stood the Flying Dutchman, Honus Wagner.

Wagner, always tough when runners were on base, slammed a drive to center field. Clarke easily made it home. Warren Gill, noting that Clarke had crossed the plate, didn't bother to touch second. He thought the game was over, so he ran to the clubhouse.

But Johnny Evers called to center fielder Art Hofman:

"Throw me the ball, Art!"

Hofman made the toss to Evers. Evers stepped on second.

"That run doesn't count," Evers complained to umpire Hank O'Day. "Gill is out."

Evers was perfectly right. The rule covering the play says:

"A run is not scored if the runner advances to home base during a play in which the third out is made (1) by

the batter-runner before he touches first base; (2) by a runner being forced out . . ."

To the dismay of Evers and his Cub mates, however, umpire O'Day said brusquely:

"I didn't see it, so I can't call it."

Cub owner Charles Webb Murphy promptly filed a protest with the League, but it was disallowed. The Cubs, bitterly disappointed, not only lost the ball game, but dropped to third place in the standings.

Just 19 days later, on September 23, the identical situation arose in a game with the Giants at the Polo Grounds. It was the third game of a four-game series. The Cubs had won the first two and the Giants were trying desperately to even things. The score was tied at 1-1 as the Giants came to bat in the last half of the ninth inning. There are different versions of what actually happened next, but the following is believed to be fairly accurate.

A Giant player named Devlin got the first hit of the inning, a single to left field. Then Moose McCormick grounded to the infield, forcing Devlin to second. Devlin went into the bag so hard he upset second baseman Evers, preventing the possibility of a double play.

A fight started at second base, but was quickly broken up by the umpires. Devlin was out.

The next Giant hitter was Fred Merkle, a quiet, modest player who showed great promise. It was his second year in the majors.

Merkle powdered the ball to deep center, and the crowd roared as Mc-

53

Joe Tinker (upper left) and Johnny Evers (lower left) were an important two-thirds of the famous Chicago Cub trio — Tinker-Evers-Chance.

Cormick streaked around the bases. He had a chance to score and end the game —or so it seemed. Cub outfielder Jack Hayden cut the ball off on a fine play and made a good throw to the infield. McCormick had to hold at third, leaving Merkle at first.

With Giant fans hooting and yelling encouragement, Al Birdwell singled sharply to center field when he came up to bat. Umpire Emslie, standing in back of second base, dropped to the ground to avoid being hit by the ball.

McCormick, of course, crossed home plate. As he did so, the gleeful Giant fans, sure their favorites had won the game, poured from their seats.

But like Pittsburgh's Warren Gill, Merkle failed to touch second. Instead he raced for the clubhouse.

Heady Johnny Evers again stepped on second and yelled to Hofman in center field.

"Throw it here! Throw it here!"

Hofman threw, but the ball got away from Evers. It rolled into the crowd surging onto the field, unaware of what was going on. Two Giants, however, must have known exactly what Evers was up to. Pitcher Floyd Kroh raced from the Giant dugout and picked up the ball. Joe McGinnity was right behind him. Before Kroh could move, McGinnity snatched the ball from Kroh's hands and heaved it into the stands.

Evers still didn't give up. He dashed to the plate and took another ball from umpire O'Day. Then he ran back to second, stepped on the bag, and insisted that Merkle was out. Umpire Emslie couldn't rule on Evers' appeal. In duck-

ing away from Birdwell's hit, he had been unable to watch Merkle. This left it up to Hank O'Day.

"What do ya say, Hank?" Merkle shouted above the noise of the screaming crowd.

"Merkle is out!" was O'Day's prompt reply. He then declared the game a tie and suspended play.

The few Giant fans who realized what had happened threatened O'Day. He had to have police protection to get to his dressing room.

The next day the president of the League upheld O'Day's ruling. The Giants quickly lodged a protest and asked for a hearing. The Cubs, to add a little more fuel to the fire, arrived at the Polo Grounds two hours earlier than the time scheduled for the fourth game of the series.

Their purpose?

"Under the rules we should play off yesterday's tie game today," Manager Chance explained to the sports writers. "And since the Giants aren't here, we claim we win by forfeiture."

The League now had *two* thorny problems to handle!

The crowd arriving with the Giants that day was in such a belligerent mood the police wouldn't permit anyone to sit close to the outfield. When the game was over, however, the Giant fans were happier. Their beloved Christy Mathewson had whipped the hateful Cubs 5 to 4.

A New York *Times* reporter gave the stay-at-homes a glimpse of the way things were at the ball park when he wrote:

In the early 1900s a Giant fan could see the games free if he was good at tree-climbing.

"Everybody slaps everybody else and nobody minds. Perfect ladies are screaming like a batch of Coney barkers on the Mardi Gras occasion and the elderly banker behind us is beating our hat to a pulp with a gold-headed cane, but nobody minds. The merry villagers flock on the field to worship the hollow where the Mathewson feet have pressed . . ."

The National League officials apparently felt that there was little chance of a tie finish in the 1908 pennant race. At least they made no move to rule on the winner of the September 23 game between the Giants and Cubs.

Later on, to everyone's astonishment, the Giants, Cubs and Pirates appeared to be heading for a triple tie! Thus, just before the season ended, the League faced up to the fact that it had to make a decision about the Merkle affair.

21. Climax!

For two days and the greater part of one night, three National League directors listened to arguments and evidence presented by the Giants and Cubs concerning the September 23 game. Finally the weary League officials ruled that Merkle was out when he failed to touch second base in the ninth inning of the game in dispute. Thus the score was 1–1. The Cubs' claim of a forfeiture was disallowed. If the tie had a bearing on the final standings, it would have to be replayed at the end of the season.

The day before the last day of the season, it became obvious that the September 23 game would have to be replayed. For on the last day the Giants were scheduled to play Boston at Boston. A victory for New York would mean a tie between the Giants and Cubs. A victory for Boston would mean a tie among the Giants, Cubs, and Pirates.

So regardless of how the Boston-Giant game ended, the replay of the 1–1 September game would have to take place.

On October 7 hundreds of Chicago fans saw the Cubs off as they boarded a special car attached to the Twentieth Century Limited. At Elkhart, Indiana— the first stop—hundreds more swarmed about the train, cheering the Cubs wildly. At departure time they refused to let the train go until Three Finger Brown, the Cubs' star hurler, went to the platform to say a few words.

As Brown finished speaking, the Elkhart station master rushed out of the station waving a piece of telegraph ticker tape.

"The Giants beat Boston! The Giants beat Boston!" he yelled.

The crowd whooped. The Twentieth Century tooted. The Cubs were off to New York for one of the most fateful games in the history of baseball.

The excitement that gripped New York as game time drew nearer and nearer was unprecedented. In the darkness of the preceding night, a dozen fans slipped into the Polo Grounds, hid among the seats, and awaited the call of "Play Ball!"

Shortly after daylight, thousands of fans from the city proper, as well as from surrounding areas, began the long trek to the Polo Grounds. A great mass of humanity—at least 80,000 and probably 100,000—tried to jam its way through the streets and into the grounds. At that time the stands seated no more than about 35,000.

Police were rushed to the area from every section of the city, but they could not control the hordes of people.

As one reporter described it:

"Thousands piled upon thousands in a fearful tangle . . . the police were swept aside like corks before a torrent. And the horses of the mounted men were pushed and jammed against the walls surrounding the grounds. . . ."

Scores of men and boys clambered over the 15-foot outfield fences, undaunted by the three strands of barbed wire that topped them. Hundreds climbed to the roof of the stands. (Two fell to the ground and were seriously injured.) Additional hundreds lined the tracks of the elevated electric trains that ran near the park.

Some spectators even scrambled up the sides of the elevated trains and sat atop them. When they wouldn't get off, the trainmen slowly moved the trains to the next station.

Excitement ran so high during the 1908 Series that the crowds broke through the fences at the Polo Grounds.

Mordecai "Three Finger" Brown, star hurler for the Cubs.

Fred Merkle, the Giant rookie who touched off the famous 1908 "incident."

According to newspaper reports of the day, several men sat along the thin, upper edge of a huge billboard that loomed above the elevated tracks. And there was a man atop each of the several thin, steel signal towers near the field. The towers were 100 feet tall.

Excitement was running high on the diamond, too. As the bell rang, ending batting practice for the Cubs, Joe McGinnity and Frank Chance became em-broiled in a hot argument. McGinnity rapped Chance on the chin. Chance retaliated, but others stepped in and separated the two.

Christy Mathewson, pitching for the Giants against Three Finger Brown, seemed in superb form as the game started.

As the fans screamed, "The fadeaway, Matty! The fadeaway!" he whiffed the first six batters he faced. But the determined Cubs rocked him in the third inning with a four-run outburst. The Giants could get only two runs from Brown.

As a result of the play-off the Cubs became the 1908 National League champions. They left the field amid a shower of pop bottles, thrown by the disappointed New York Giant fans.

In the clubhouse Merkle wept with shame. Over and over again he said to Giant manager McGraw:

"Get rid of me, Mac! Get rid of me! I don't deserve to play with the Giants!"

But McGraw, toughest of the tough, a manager who was supposed to be heartless, patted Merkle on the shoulder and said gruffly:

"Forget it, Fred. As of right now you've got a $500 raise."

For years afterward, however, the fans hooted at Merkle when he appeared on the field. And whenever anyone made a foolish mistake, it was often referred to as "a Merkle."

22. The Big Train

The pennant races of 1908, torrid as they were, didn't capture all the headlines that memorable year. As always, there were a number of remarkable individual performances.

The most amazing of these was turned in by a pitcher for the seventh-place Washington Senators, Walter Perry Johnson.

Johnson, rounding out his first full year in the majors, shut out the Highlanders 3–0 on September 4, a Friday. He also shut them out on Saturday, 6–0. Since the law didn't permit the playing of professional ball on Sunday, the teams were idle. On Monday Johnson was back on the mound for the final game of the series. This time he whipped New York 4–0. In all, Johnson had given up but 12 hits. On September 11 he pitched

"No mere mortal" could throw a baseball as hard as the newcomer from Idaho—Walter P. Johnson.

59

the Senators to a 2–1 victory over the Athletics. The next day, he beat them again by a 5–4 score.

When Johnson had arrived in Washington during August of 1907, he was not unknown. No one can strike out an average of 20 batters a game, as Johnson did in the Idaho State League, without attracting attention. The stories circulated about Johnson, however, were so extravagant with praise that few believed them.

Even those who saw him make his debut with the Senators scarcely trusted their senses. As one awed sports reporter wrote:

"No mere mortal can throw a baseball as hard as the newcomer from Idaho. I have seen him pitch, but I do not believe what I have seen. My eyes speak falsehoods."

In a way, Johnson's great speed caused him to lose his first game for the Senators. The opposing Detroit Tigers, unable to hit his lightning-like deliveries, cleverly resorted to bunting and were able to eke out a 3–2 victory.

Ty Cobb, who led the attack against Johnson that day, said later:

"The most terrible experience in baseball is to visit Washington on a cloudy day when Johnson is pitching."

On another occasion, after striking out against Johnson, Cobb muttered:

"You can't hit what you can't see."

In 21 seasons with the Senators, Walter Johnson established 15 records—more than any other pitcher. These included the most games won (413), the most shutouts (113), the most innings pitched (5,925) and the most consecutive scoreless innings (56).

Johnson, a powerful square-shouldered man with strong features, was likened to the giant steam locomotives of his day.

"The Big Train is coming to town," wrote a sports writer when Johnson and the Senators traveled to New York. And "The Big Train" he remained to all as he rolled on, year after glorious year.

23. Color and Competition

One might think that interest in baseball would have faded after a year like 1908. Actually the turnstiles spun at a merrier rate than ever for the next several seasons.

There were many reasons for this. First of all, the American and National League franchises were left undisturbed. This gave the teams a chance to build a loyal home following which, in turn, led to intense rivalries between cities.

As fan interest grew, so did the prestige of baseball. In 1910 William Howard Taft became the first President of the United States to toss out the ball that opened the season. The President and all the other Washington rooters were thrilled by Walter Johnson's per-

William Howard Taft, the first President of the United States to toss out the season's opening ball.

formance that day. He just missed pitching a no-hit game. Taft became an outspoken admirer of Johnson, as did Presidents Harding and Wilson in later years.

Although still poorly paid, the players responded to the rooting of their loyal followers by putting on a spectacular show. The Cincinnati Reds, for example, stole 310 bases in 1910 even though the manufacturers had added cork to the center of the baseball to make it more lively. The Reds' leading base stealer was Bob Bescher with a record of 80. The National League, as a whole, recorded 1,691 stolen bases!

Ty Cobb led the American League with 76 stolen bases. But despite the efforts of Cobb and Bescher, neither the Tigers nor the Reds won pennants that year.

Instead, the American League championship was taken by the Athletics, who won 102 games. The Athletics were the first American League team to go over the 100-win mark. In fact in 1910 they were one of the finest teams in baseball. Brilliant Eddie Collins led the A's attack with a .322 batting average and 67 stolen bases (second to Cobb).

Collins was also the middle man in baseball's best infield. Referred to as the "$100,000 infield," it included Frank Baker, Stuffy McInnis, Jack Barry, and Harry Davis.

The pitching, too, was very strong. Together, Jack Coombs and Charles "Chief" Bender won 54 games. Coombs had 13 shutouts among his 31 victories. Eddie Plank, although getting along in years, won 16 games.

The Cubs won the National League pennant, but they were no match for the Athletics in the 1910 World Series play. They lost by a score of 4–1.

The following year the Giants virtually "stole" the pennant by stealing a record total of 347 bases. Such a display of footwork is not without hazard, however. As the season progressed, the Giants' uniforms became more and more tattered and worn. Finally, during a game in Chicago, it happened. A Giant slid into second and couldn't get up. His pants were no longer on his body. A cordon of teammates led him from the field to the whooping delight of the fans.

That same year, 1911, Ty Cobb led the American League again with 83 stolen bases. He also batted a phenomenal .420 and scored 147 runs. Still his team couldn't match the Athletics. The Tigers trailed by 13½ games. The Athletics had a .400 hitter of their own that year—Shoeless Joe Jackson. Jackson, one of the best hitters ever to grace the diamond, batted .411.

When the Giants and Athletics met in the World Series, the fans became conscious of a new weapon of attack—the home run.

It didn't show itself in the first game when the Giants bested the Athletics 2–1 in a bitterly fought contest. But in the second game it exploded against Rube Marquard. Marquard, who had won 24 games for the Giants, gave up but four hits during the game. But unfortunately one of them was the homer which rang off the bat of Frank Baker, giving the ball game to the Athletics.

The Giants' Christy Mathewson and

In 1910-11 nobody in the American League managed to steal more bases than Ty Cobb.

the Athletics' Jack Coombs dueled away in the third game. In the ninth inning, with the score tied at 1–1, Baker came to bat. Matty, working carefully, slipped two strikes past the third baseman. He wound up and fired again.

Baker swung and seemed to miss the ball. But the umpire ruled that Baker's bat had touched it. This gave Baker another chance. He promptly belted Matty's next pitch into the stands. Although the Giants evened matters in the bottom of the ninth, they lost in the eleventh

when the A's scored another run.

Baker hit still a third homer as the Athletics went on to win the Series. This unheard-of feat earned for him the nickname "Home Run Baker."

In 1912 the pennant races continued to whet the fans' appetite for baseball, especially in the American League. Ty Cobb, hated as much as admired, drew cheers and jeers in an ever rising crescendo. The jeers finally got out of hand. In a hotly fought series in New York on May 15, Cobb astounded everyone by

The captains of the Braves and Athletics have a conference with the umpires at the start of the 1914 World Series.

leaping into the stands to grab a fan by the throat and pummel him.

"He insulted me," Cobb explained later.

This didn't satisfy Ban Johnson, who sent a wire to the Detroit management: "Cobb suspended indefinitely."

Cobb's teammates, knowing what he meant to the club, sent a telegram back to Johnson. They said they would strike if Cobb's suspension wasn't lifted.

Johnson, never one to be bluffed, had a ready reply. If the players struck,

Detroit would be fined $5,000 for each game not played.

The players struck anyway when the team was scheduled to play in Philadelphia. Hughie Jennings, the manager, to keep the schedule, put himself into the lineup along with his coaches and a group of college players. The game was a farce, of course. The Athletics won 24–2.

The next day's game was canceled, but Cobb begged his mates to resume playing, which they did. Each man who signed the telegram was fined $100, while Cobb's suspension lasted 10 days and was capped by a $50 fine.

Meanwhile, the Boston Red Sox and Washington Senators were stirring up even more excitement in the American League.

Walter Johnson, pitching for a relatively weak team, won 32 games while losing 16. During one stretch he won 16 in a row as the Senators moved from sixth place to second.

The Boston club, a real powerhouse, rolled up 104 wins to take the flag. Boston pitcher Smoky Joe Wood also won 16 in a row that year and wound up with a total of 34 wins and 5 losses. Unlike Johnson, Wood had the backing of a remarkable outfield in Tris Speaker, Duffy Lewis, and Harry Hooper. This trio could field and hit with the best that baseball has ever seen.

In the National League, meanwhile, John McGraw's Giants won still another pennant. The World Series was a great climax to the season, with the Red Sox winning 4–3.

The following year Connie Mack added two remarkable rookies to his pitching staff—Bullet Joe Bush and Herb Pennock. The additions meant another Athletic pennant.

The still superb Christy Mathewson and Rube Marquard (who won 19 in a row) led the Giants to the flag in the National League. But in the World Series play the A's again downed the Giants, this time 4–1. The lone Giant victory went to Mathewson.

The Athletics repeated their pennant victory in 1914, but they didn't have such an easy time in the World Series. Instead of the Giants, they encountered a "miracle team," the Boston Braves.

Managed by George Stallings, the Braves astounded everyone by moving from last place in mid-July to a pennant victory in September.

The Braves, a "hot" ball club, rolled over the A's in four straight games, the first time this had ever been accomplished in World Series play.

The star of the Series was the Braves' Hank Gowdy, who batted .545 with a homer, triple, and three doubles. He also collected six walks from the jittery Athletic pitchers.

The close of the 1914 season marked the climax of a prosperous era. Intercity rivalries and color and competition had made it so.

24. The "Feds"

In 1913 baseball's comfortable financial position suddenly began to be threatened from several directions at once. Some two million Americans were spending their free time with a noisy, unreliable contraption called a motor car, or "horseless buggy." Thousands of others were drawn to the "electric theater," where they could watch moving pictures tell fascinating stories.

Still more serious was the formation of the Federal League by a group of wealthy businessmen. Within three months, the Feds built eight new ball parks. Many were in cities where the National and American League teams had franchises.

To get players, the Federal League owners followed the patterns of the past. They offered the established stars more money than they were receiving. Three Finger Brown, Joe Tinker, Ed Reulbach and Hal Chase were among many who jumped to the Federal League.

Surprisingly enough, the Feds put on a fine show in 1914, their first season. Indianapolis nosed out Chicago for the pennant, but every team was in contention at one time or another. The closeness of the race drew big crowds.

Encouraged by such a fine start, the Federals got bolder in 1915 and moved the Indianapolis franchise to Newark. They also continued to lure players from

65

Charles "Chief" Bender, one of the Athletics' star pitchers, transferred to the new Federal League in 1915.

the National and American loops, including Chief Bender and Eddie Plank.

The flag chase that year was even more exciting than the year before. Chicago, St. Louis, and Pittsburgh fought it out right down to the wire with the rest of the League close behind. Chicago won by one percentage point.

By the time the Boston Red Sox met Philadelphia of the National League in the World Series, there were reports that the Federals were going to move into New York for 1916. Because of all the competition from automobiles, movies, and the Federal League, attendance had fallen off for the first time in years.

Just when things were blackest, the Federal League owners—men used to getting their own way—had a quarrel. Then their richest and most powerful member, Robert Ward, died unexpectedly.

The American and National Leagues quickly bid for peace. After a number of conferences, they bought out the Federal League franchises, throwing the players on the open market.

Two important ownership changes followed the breakup of the Federal League. One of the Federal owners—Charles Weeghman—bought the Chicago Cubs, then built Wrigley Field for them.

In New York two colonels—Jacob Ruppert and Tillinghast L'Hommedieu Huston—purchased the American League team known as the Highlanders. The Highlanders, however, were soon to become much better known under a new name, The Yankees.

25. From White to Black

World War I had an inevitable effect on baseball. Many of the leading ball players joined the ranks of the doughboys sailing for the battlefront in France. Even so, baseball was able to continue. And in 1918, during the closing months of the war, the Boston Red Sox whipped the Chicago Cubs 4–2 in World Series play.

By the spring of 1919, baseball, like the rest of the world, began to get back to normal. The Chicago White Sox, boasting the most powerful lineup in the major leagues, rolled easily to a pennant in the American League, while a less imposing club, the Cincinnati Reds, took the National League flag.

Ed Cicotte was the leading pitcher of the White Sox with 29 victories and 7 losses. Others who contributed heavily to the championship drive of the Chicago team were Ray Schalk, catcher, outfielders Shoeless Joe Jackson and Oscar "Happy" Felsch, and pitchers Claude "Lefty" Williams and Dickie Kerr. Then there was Charles "Swede" Risberg at shortstop, Chick Gandil, first baseman, and George "Buck" Weaver, third baseman. Pilot of the Sox was William "Kid" Gleason, a member of the original Baltimore Orioles.

As Cincinnati and Chicago squared off for the best-of-nine series in Cincinnati, baseball fans were startled to learn that the Reds were favored to win the opening game and the Series. Many of the reporters who were in Cincinnati to begin coverage of the Series immediately became suspicious, not only because the Reds were favored, but also because known gamblers were circulating through the lobby of the White Sox' hotel, trying to find anyone willing to bet on Chicago.

Long before game time, there were ominous whispers.

"The Series is fixed," was the word among those who knew.

In the first game, the talented Cicotte was matched against the Reds' ace hurler, Dutch Ruether. Ruether got the Sox out without a score as the game opened. In the bottom of the first inning, however, Cicotte hit the first batter. Before the inning was over, the Reds had scored.

"What's the matter with Cicotte?" the Chicago fans wondered. "He's just lobbing the ball up there."

"He's nervous," some said aloud.

Cicotte, however, couldn't seem to settle down. In the fourth inning, the first batter flied out, the second singled, and the third was thrown out on a fielder's choice. With two outs, two singles followed, putting men on second and third. This brought to the plate the Reds' weakest hitter, pitcher Dutch Ruether.

Ruether whacked out a triple. A double and single followed, running the score to 6–1 and sending Cicotte to the showers. Before the game was over, the Reds scored three more runs and won the first game 9–1.

Kid Gleason of the White Sox had heard the whispers about a "fix" before

67

Record-breaking crowds thronged to watch the 1919 World Series games between the Chicago White Sox and Cincinnati Reds.

game time, but he couldn't believe them. By the end of the game he was convinced they were true. He called the players together and gave them a tongue-lashing. Later he went to owner Charles Comiskey and told him of his suspicions.

Comiskey and Gleason talked far into the night. They decided there was nothing to be done about the first game. After all, whom could they accuse? What evidence did they have?

The second game gave them little comfort, for Chicago lost again, 4–2. As the teams moved to Chicago for the third game, the "fix" rumors increased. Still Comiskey and Gleason were helpless.

Little Dickie Kerr almost made Gleason and Comiskey forget their dark suspicions. Hurling a masterful game, he whipped the Reds 3–0. The next day Cicotte begged Gleason for another chance to pitch against Cincinnati. Gleason hesitated, but finally decided to give Cicotte the assignment.

He was disappointed. Cicotte made two bad errors in the fifth inning, paving the way for a 2–0 Cincinnati victory.

Were the errors intentional, or natural?

Gleason couldn't be sure.

The fifth game was delayed a day because of rain. It was a long day for Gleason and Comiskey, tortured by the thought that their wonderful White Sox were crooked.

With Lefty Williams on the mound the next day, the White Sox lost the fifth game. Errors and all-around poor play by Felsch and Risberg gave Cincinnati the win.

The teams moved back to Cincinnati and Dick Kerr again was called on to face the Reds. He won a close one in 10 innings. Though still worried about Cicotte, Gleason asked him to pitch a third time. Cicotte was at his best. Timely hits by Jackson and Felsch gave the Sox a 4–1 victory and kept their Series hopes alive, although they trailed 4 games to 3.

The Reds crushed Chicago the next day, however, pounding Lefty Williams for four runs in the first inning. The final score was 10–5.

At the end of the Series, Charles Comiskey said he thought his players were honest. Nevertheless, he offered a $20,000 reward for any information that could prove the Series was fixed. He also held up the Sox share of the World Series money temporarily.

No one made any attempt to claim Comiskey's reward during the winter months. By the following season the incident seemed to be forgotten.

In September, however, Chicago's Cook County Grand Jury was instructed to look into rumors that a game between the Chicago Cubs and the Philadelphia Phillies was fixed. Some of the developments touched on the Cincinnati-Chicago World Series of the year before.

Suddenly an ex-prize fighter and small-time gambler named Billy Maharg blurted out a fantastic story to a newspaperman. He said the World Series of 1919 had definitely been rigged. He named the players involved and gave facts and figures.

The Grand Jury, acting swiftly, called a number of people to testify. Unex-

White Sox player Buck Weaver out at home plate during a play of the 1919 Series.

pectedly Ed Cicotte came forward as a voluntary witness. Here, in substance, is apparently what happened:

Maharg and another man, acting upon the instructions of certain gamblers, contacted the players through first baseman Chick Gandil. They offered eight of the Sox $100,000 to lose the Series. The eight included Cicotte, Gandil, Joe Jackson, Lefty Williams, Swede Risberg, Happy Felsch, Buck Weaver and Fred McMullin.

Cicotte, who later said he needed money to pay off a mortgage on his farm, found $10,000 under his pillow after the first game. Williams, Jackson, and Felsch had been promised $20,000 each, but they received only $5,000 apiece. The others received nothing.

Shortly after Cicotte gave his story to the Grand Jury, Williams, Felsch, and Jackson told of their part in the plot. As the famous Jackson left the courthouse, a group of boys clustered about him. One, with tears streaming down his face, said:

"Say it ain't so, Joe! Say it ain't so!"

The slugging outfielder, idol of a million youngsters, flushed and hung his head. "I'm afraid it is, boys," he murmured, then hurried away.

When the ugly story broke, the Cleveland Indians were leading the Sox by one game, with three left to be played. Nonetheless, the eight implicated White Sox players were suspended. Cleveland won the pennant and the World Series, beating Brooklyn 5–2.

The Grand Jury also indicted nine players implicated in the Cubs-Phillies case. Four gamblers were indicted, too. The case didn't go to trial until the following year. At that time, it was discovered that the Grand Jury minutes, including the testimony of all the witnesses, had been stolen from the prosecutor's office.

As a result, the Grand Jury had no choice but to return a verdict of Not Guilty against all involved. Although exonerated by the court, the White Sox players were barred from baseball for life.

For years writers have been trying to unravel all that went on during the 1919 Series. Long after the incident, Ban Johnson said two groups of gamblers were involved, each trying to double-cross the other. The players were caught in between. No scandal in sports history shocked the public so much as the White Sox affair of 1919. The club owners were aware of this and decided they had better do something about it.

By coincidence August Herrmann had resigned as chairman of the National Commission, and baseball was without a supreme leader in 1920. The owners, over Ban Johnson's protests, picked Judge Kenesaw Mountain Landis as his successor. Landis was well known as a stern, courageous, and fair judge. During the war between the Federal League and the National and American Leagues, he had said:

Judge Kenesaw Mountain Landis was appointed commissioner of baseball shortly after the White Sox scandal of 1919.

"Both sides may understand that any blow at the thing called baseball would be regarded by this court as a blow to a national institution."

Landis was given the title of commissioner of baseball with a salary of $50,-000 a year. More power was put into his hands than any other baseball man had ever had.

The team owners were determined that the crookedness that changed the White Sox to the Black Sox would never happen again.

26. Rejuvenation

The severe blow dealt baseball by the Black Sox scandal was softened somewhat by the appointment of Kenesaw Mountain Landis as czar of the game. But Judge Landis wasn't a gate attraction—he couldn't hit, field, or pitch. Above all, the game needed something or someone to bring the fans streaming back to the parks as in the years before the Federal League war.

Magically, baseball found the answer to all its ills in the powerful bat of a moon-faced kid from Baltimore, George Herman Ruth.

Babe Ruth, as he came to be known to millions the world over, was born in Baltimore on February 6, 1895, one of eight children. His father owned a cheap barroom, where George was required to do chores. With both his father and mother working long hours, George found plenty of time to get into trouble. He became so uncontrollable that his parents sent him to St. Mary's Industrial School for Boys. He was seven years old when he first entered. By the time he was 19, he had been in and out of the school five times.

St. Mary's was a poor and struggling institution. But life there was good for George in many ways. It brought his wild nature under some degree of control. And it gave him the opportunity of playing baseball on an organized team.

George Ruth's first tutor was Brother Mathias, a considerate, kind man who understood boys and knew how to handle them.

Brother Mathias saw many good qualities in George, although others had branded him an incorrigible. Like almost any boy, George responded to kindness and understanding. He worked hard at learning his trade—that of a shirtmaker. He also worked hard at learning how to play baseball.

George Ruth had another friend at St. Mary's—Brother Gilbert, head of the school. Fortunately for George, Brother Gilbert was friendly with Jack Dunn, owner of the Baltimore Orioles.

When Ruth was 19, Brother Gilbert told Dunn about the boy.

"He's got great potential as a pitcher," Brother Gilbert said. "I wish you'd take a look at him."

One look was enough for Dunn.

"I'll take him," he said.

But since Ruth had been committed to St. Mary's by the courts, Dunn had to agree that he would be responsible for the youth's conduct until he was 21. This he did, and in February of 1914 Ruth, nervous and apprehensive, left St. Mary's for the Orioles' training camp.

When owner Jack Dunn first put a Baltimore uniform on the youngster, one of the Orioles slapped his leg with glee and shouted:

"Look! Here's another one of Dunn's babes!"

In his first intra-squad game, the Babe hit the longest homer ever seen in the Oriole training camp. But it wasn't the home run that impressed his manager. It was the way the rookie could pitch.

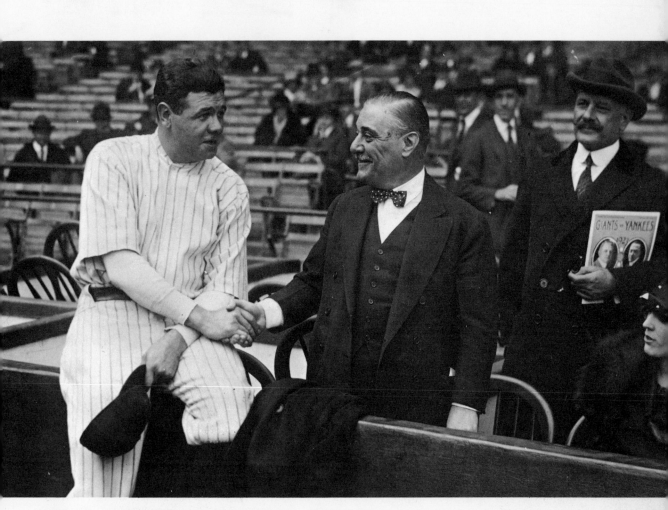

Babe Ruth shakes hands with his boss, Colonel Jacob Ruppert, co-owner of the Yankees.

As the Orioles ran through their schedule in the early part of the season, Ruth began to rack up one win after another.

The Orioles were in trouble, though, despite the presence of the bright young rookie. For that was the year the Federal League moved a team into Baltimore. Jack Dunn began to lose money trying to compete. Finally he had no choice but to sell off some of his players. Ruth, Ernie Shore, and Ben Egan went to the Boston Red Sox for less than $10,000.

Ruth hit his first major league home run in the Polo Grounds on May 6, 1915, as a rookie pitcher for the Red Sox. He banged out three more that season. In 1917 he hit but two.

Ruth was not only a good hitter but also one of the best base stealers on the club. Manager Ed Barrow wanted him in the lineup every day. When not pitching, Ruth went to the outfield.

Ruth's hitting, however, didn't begin to draw the attention of the fans until 1919. That year he hit 29 homers, breaking the record of 27 set by Ed Williamson in 1884. Baseball officials were quick to see the effect the home run had on the fans. They gave more life to the ball for the 1920 season.

But Ruth was no longer in a Red Sox uniform when he started the 1920 season. During the winter months Red Sox owner Harry Frazee, badly in debt, offered Ruth to the New York Yankees for $100,000 in cash and a loan of $385,000. The two Colonels—Ruppert and Huston —accepted the offer, and the biggest player transaction in baseball history went through.

Once seen the Ruthian homer was never forgotten.

There was one little hitch before Ruth put on his new uniform. To the delight of fans everywhere, Ruth announced that the Yankees would have to increase his salary.

"Yep," he told the astonished colonels, "you've got to double it."

The colonels swallowed hard, but gave Ruth a contract for $20,000.

For the first two weeks of the season, Ruth looked like a poor investment. He didn't get a single hit. But his sights were adjusted by May 1, when he hit his first homer. By July he had passed his 1919 record of 29. And at the end of the season he had lashed out a staggering total of 54—25 more than his own record and 27 more than any other player in the entire history of the game! In addition, he batted .376 to lead the League.

The fans talked of him endlessly— about his personality, his every move on the diamond. For Ruth was unique in many ways. Although a big man, he stood at the plate with his feet close together, toes turned inward slightly. His body was straight from the waist down. From the waist up, he leaned forward a bit.

From the stands it appeared that Ruth was listening to something that was going on behind him as he waited for the pitch. His head would be cocked to the right and held rock-still.

Ruth used one of the biggest bats in the majors—42 ounces. Nevertheless he held it at the end, which was unusual in his day. As he waited for the pitch, the bat would be pointed skyward, well to the left of his left shoulder. Usually the fat end moved in a slow circle. It re-minded a spectator of the way a cat twitches its tail before pouncing on a mouse.

Once seen, the Ruthian homer was never forgotten. Most home-run hitters power the ball into the seats or over the wall on either a line or a high arc. But Ruth's hits soared lazily skyward to dizzying heights, then carried farther and farther from the plate. When they dropped, they seemed to drop straight down. Even the shots that stayed in the park often amazed the fans. Once Ruth hit a fly to the infield. It went so high that Jimmy Dykes got dizzy circling around beneath it. The ball fell in back of Dykes and, by the time he had recovered it, Ruth was standing on second.

The Yankees, playing at the Polo Grounds, outdrew their landlords, the Giants, by a wide margin. As a matter of fact, they established an attendance record of 1,289,422. It wasn't topped until 26 years later.

Why did the fans flock to wherever the Yankees played? To see Babe Ruth.

The impact the round-faced slugger made on the game is still evident today.

27. A Pennant for the Yankees

Babe Ruth was no ordinary man on the diamond. He was no ordinary man off it, either. Baseball has never known a wilder, more carefree, fun-loving, free-spending, big-hearted player. Neither has it known a player loved by so many, especially by boys and girls.

Ruth burst upon the baseball scene when America seemed bent on living wildly. It was the start of a period known as "The Roaring Twenties." As the 1921 season ran its course, Babe Ruth seemed to set the pace for the topsy-turvy world. He fought openly with pint-sized Miller Huggins, his manager. He consistently broke training. He deliberately ignored front-office rules.

When the team was traveling, for example, the players were assigned hotel rooms that cost about $3 a day. Ruth moved into suites that cost $100 a day. If the team traveled to Boston, or Washington, or Philadelphia by train—Ruth would go by car. Once, as he raced between Philadelphia and Washington, his car overturned on the treacherous roads. Miraculously he escaped with but minor injuries.

Ruth's mode of living didn't seem to affect his playing that year. He hit 59 homers, batted .378 and knocked in 170 runs. He led the League in RBIs and homers. More important, he paced the New York Yankees to their first American League championship.

And what team did the New York Yankees have to face in the 1921 World Series? Dramatically enough, it was another New York team—the Giants.

John McGraw, cocky and combative as ever, couldn't wait to get at the Yankees, a team that had stolen his public—and right in his own ball park.

McGraw got his vengeance, too. His proud Giants whipped the upstart Yankees 5–3.

Yankee fans had a ready alibi. Ruth hadn't played in the last three games because of an injury. The Giants hooted at this. One sports writer even went so far as to hint that Ruth was faking. When Ruth read the story, he became so angry he tried to force his way into the press box and attack the writer.

Still smarting from the crushing defeat at the hands of the Giants, Ruth took on another opponent after the Series ended. It was Judge Landis.

In the view of Judge Kenesaw Mountain Landis, the rules of the National Commission, which governed all of professional baseball, were not to be broken by anyone. And that included George Herman Ruth, the biggest sports personality in America.

Ruth had a different opinion. When the 1921 World Series ended, he announced that he and teammates Bob Meusel and Bill Piercy were going on a barnstorming trip. Each man was to receive $1,000 a day. Judge Landis pointed out that the rules forbade players from participating in baseball games once the season closed.

"The heck with the old goat," Ruth said. "I'm not under contract and if I want to play ball, I'll play ball!"

Meusel and Piercy agreed, and the three went ahead with their plans. They were soon to regret it.

Not only did the tour fail after six days, but Judge Landis showed the boys he was not to be trifled with.

He ordered the players' World Series shares, which amounted to about $3,000 each, held back. He also suspended them for the first 40 days of the following season.

Both the Yankee management and Ban Johnson, president of the American League, as well as press and public, were stunned by the severity of the Landis ruling. All of them set up a thunderous howl.

The Yankees and the American League pointed out that Ruth was baseball's biggest attraction. To keep him out of the lineup for a whole month might cost them thousands of dollars.

"He can't do this!" was the cry heard from every side.

Landis stood firm.

With Ruth and Meusel out of uniform, the Yankees floundered badly during the spring. And even after the players rejoined the club, everything went wrong.

Ruth and his mates created most of the trouble themselves. They fought with each other. They refused to obey training rules. In short, they did about

The fun-loving Babe poses with the four-year-old Yankee mascot, little Ray Kelly.

A handshake marks the end of one of Ruth's many feuds with manager Miller Huggins.

everything athletes should *not* do. Ed Barrow, general manager of the Yankees, and Miller Huggins tried mightily to bring the team to its senses. And somehow the New Yorkers finally managed to win their second pennant. They slipped into the 1922 championship one game ahead of Cleveland.

But although they won the pennant, the Yankees failed to capture the big prize, the World Series. And it was the New York Giants, to the utter delight of John McGraw, who kept it from them. The Giants whipped the Yankees in four of five games! (One game ended in a tie.)

As for Ruth, he had the poorest Series record ever. He batted a lowly .118, gaining but two hits in 17 trips to the plate.

The Ruth suspension and the World Series whipping at the hands of the Giants taught the Yankees a much-needed lesson.

28. New Seeds

New names pop into baseball every year. Some disappear quickly. Others remain and become a part of the great legend of the game. While Babe Ruth blazed a new record with his booming homers, a serious, intelligent, and ambitious man named Branch Rickey was moving into the limelight.

Rickey had paid his way through Ohio Wesleyan with earnings from playing football and baseball. He made the majors in 1905, and was purchased by the Cincinnati Reds after two seasons as a catcher at Dallas.

But the Reds got rid of Rickey because he refused to play ball on Sunday. He was signed then by the New York Highlanders and later by the St. Louis Browns.

Branch Rickey was a competent player but not a great one. Soon he became interested in managing—both on the field and in the front office. Before World War I, he managed the Browns. In 1919, he took over as pilot of the St. Louis Cardinals. The Cardinals were a last-place club, badly in debt with little prospect of being able to do anything about it.

During the season the New York Giants became interested in Rogers Hornsby, the only really valuable ball player the Cardinals had under contract. Manager John McGraw and Charles Stoneham, a new Giant owner, paid Rickey a visit.

"We'll give you five Giant players for Hornsby," McGraw said.

Rickey smiled and said nothing.

McGraw then added a sum of cash to the offer.

Rickey still showed no interest.

Soon Stoneham took over the bidding. He offered Rickey the five players and $100,000 for Hornsby. He went to $125,000, then $150,000. As the bidding went on, McGraw drew up a lineup for Rickey to show him how the five Giant players could be used.

Though Stoneham finally offered $250,000 along with the five players, Rickey was unmoved.

"Rogers Hornsby is the only great ball player I've got and I can't sell him," was Rickey's attitude. The deal fell through.

Rickey soon had occasion to regret his decision—at least temporarily. Hornsby, driving into second on the front end of a double play, was hit on the head by a thrown ball. He had to be carried from the field on a stretcher.

Luckily Hornsby recovered. He went on to become the greatest right-handed batter the game has ever seen, leading his league six straight times. During 22 years in the majors, Hornsby batted over .400 four times. Once he hit .424, the highest average ever attained by a modern player. His lifetime average of .358 is topped only by Ty Cobb.

The shock of seeing Hornsby almost killed by a thrown ball gave Branch Rickey plenty of food for thought. He realized that it was dangerous to bank so heavily on a single player. What he

A thoughtful Rogers Hornsby waits for his turn at bat.

needed was not one Rogers Hornsby, but a dozen.

Since rosters of major league clubs are limited, Rickey conceived the idea of placing players in the minor league teams, where they could be controlled and trained. With the backing of owner Sam Breadon, he began stocking several minor league teams with a great corps of untried rookies.

The Cards, chiefly because of Rickey's foresight, moved from last place in 1919 to a tie for third place in 1922. They then suffered a slump, but later went on to their greatest period of glory.

The year the Cardinals tied for third place was the same season the Giants humiliated the Yankees in World Series play. It was also the year Rickey saw one of his St. Louis players win the American League's Most Valuable Player Award. The player was George Sisler. He had a .420 batting average and 51 stolen bases.

Although hampered by eye trouble, Sisler batted .340 during his 15 years in the majors. He was considered to be almost as good a hitter as Hornsby.

By 1922 the Giants had added many new names to the growing list of stars playing in the majors. Among them was a graduate of Fordham University, Frank Frisch. Frisch, who started at third base, then moved to second, could easily have been included among the tough Orioles of the 1880s. He would have been right at home alongside John McGraw and Hughie Jennings, for he played baseball as though he were playing for his life. He was tough, courageous, and skillful.

About this time the Giants acquired another McGraw type of player—a scrawny, scrappy outfielder who started his adult life as a left-handed dentist. The new outfielder, Charles Dillon Stengel, loved to win ball games. He also delighted McGraw by keeping him company at all hours of the night as he talked about baseball.

Stengel, nicknamed "Casey" because he hailed from Kansas City, warmed the hearts of Giant fans in the 1923 Series against the Yankees. In each of two games, he hit homers to give the Giants a victory. As he circled the bases after hitting the second one, the brash youngster thumbed his nose at the Yankee

bench. Little did he realize that some-
day he would be sitting on that bench
building baseball's greatest managerial
record.

The Yankees of 1923, however, were
not to be underestimated. They started
the year with a different attitude and in
a new home, Yankee Stadium.

Babe Ruth, always able to rise to the
occasion, christened the stadium in true
Ruthian style. With two men on base,
he hit a homer, giving the Yankees a 4–2
victory. His home run started them toward their third pennant. In World Series play, the mighty Yanks revenged the
crushing defeat of the year before,
downing the Giants 4–2. Ruth, who won
the homer title with 41, made up for his
terrible 1922 showing by crashing out
three homers, a triple, double, and three
singles. This performance, plus his .393
season average, won him the Most Valuable Player award. He was the first Yankee to earn that distinction.

Although Ruth led the American
League home-run parade again in 1924,
the Yankees finished second to the Washington Senators. And with the Senators'
victory, the name of Stanley Raymond
"Bucky" Harris burst into prominence.

Harris, the Senators' second baseman,
took over as manager of the team after
several others had failed to pull the ball
club together. Dubbed "The Boy Wonder," Harris handled the club with great
skill, leading it from seventh place to the
pennant.

Harris, of course, was blessed with one
of the finest pitchers in the game—Walter Johnson. Although past his prime,
Johnson worked as never before. In the

*A new Giant star, Frank Frisch, who played
baseball for all he was worth.*

stretch drive as the Senators fought to
overtake the Yankees, Johnson won 11 in
a row. He finished the season with a
23–7 record.

Washington's opponent in the 1924
World Series was the tough New York
Giants. Although Harris realized Johnson was worn out by the pennant fight,
he gave the big pitcher the opening-
game assignment. Johnson pitched well,
but the Senators lost 4 to 3 in 12 innings.
Johnson also lost the fifth game 6–2. In
the twelfth inning of the seventh game,
the score was tied when one of the Senators hit a hot drive. The ball struck a
pebble in front of the Giants' third baseman, Freddy Lindstrom, and bounded

81

The fabulous Waner brothers—Paul and Lloyd.

over his head. That freakish bounce gave the Senators their first World Series.

The following year, Johnson gave his all again, winning 20 and losing 7 as he paced the Senators to still another pennant. This time the Senators met the Pittsburgh Pirates in the Series.

Like the Pirates of 1960, the Pittsburgh club of 1925 was built around youngsters, among them talented Paul Waner. (Lloyd Waner joined Paul in the outfield the next year. So potent were their bats, they were referred to as "Big Poison" and "Little Poison.") Pacing the Pirates' attack was Harold "Pie" Traynor, often rated the game's best third baseman. Traynor batted .320. This was his average for the 17 years he played in the majors.

The Pirate-Washington Series went to seven games—the same number as the year before. But it seemed to have more thrills. Walter Johnson, the sentimental favorite of fans everywhere, won the first and fourth games by scores of 4–1 and 4–0. But he lost the seventh game 9–7 as Roger Peckinpaugh made eight errors, two of them letting in four runs.

It was Johnson's last World Series and his next-to-last season. In spring training in 1927, a batting-practice line drive broke his ankle, ending his career.

Lou Gehrig impressed everyone with the ferocious way he could hit a baseball.

29. The Iron Horse

On June 2, 1925, the New York Yankees' veteran first baseman, Wally Pipp, had to leave a game because of a headache. He was replaced by a rookie who had played in his first Yankee game the day before. The rookie's name was Henry Louis Gehrig.

Pipp next played first base a year later, and in another league. When Gehrig took over from Pipp, he started a consecutive game-playing streak that in all probability will never be broken. In a span of 14 years, he played in 2,130 consecutive games!

Gehrig, who had played both football and baseball in high school, came from a poor, hard-working family. After Lou graduated from high school, he and his mother and father worked in a fraternity house at Columbia University, where Gehrig had enrolled. Lou waited on table, while his mother cooked and his father did the house maintenance work.

While at Columbia, Gehrig was given a workout at the Polo Grounds under the watchful eye of John McGraw. The big, square-shouldered college boy immediately impressed McGraw with the ferocious way he could hit a baseball.

The wily McGraw sent Gehrig to Hartford, a Class A team in the Eastern League. He told Gehrig to play under the name of "Lewis," so he could protect his amateur standing and remain eligible for sports at Columbia. Columbia officials learned of the trick, however, and quickly persuaded Gehrig to leave Hartford.

The next year, while pitching for Columbia against Rutgers University, Gehrig hit two long home runs. Columbia won by a score of 9–4. A Yankee scout saw the game, raced to a phone, and called the Yankee front office.

"I've found another Ruth!" he cried.

Gehrig signed a contract with the Yankees in 1923. He was then farmed out to Hartford, where he played about a third of the season and hit 24 homers. The next year he went to spring training with the Yankees, but was returned to Hartford where he batted .368 and hit 37 homers. When the Eastern League season closed, Gehrig rejoined the Yankees and there he stayed.

Lou Gehrig, always quiet and dignified, disciplined himself and worked hard at his trade. Even after he became a star, he continued to try to improve and never held himself above correction or instruction.

Like Babe Ruth, Lou Gehrig's feats on the diamond have filled the record books. In each of 13 seasons, he knocked in 100 or more runs. His lifetime average was .340 over a 17-year span. In his total of 2,721 hits, he had 493 homers, 161 triples and 535 doubles. Twenty-three of Gehrig's homers came with the bases loaded. On three occasions he hit three homers in a row in single games. In one game he hit four in a row.

With Gehrig batting behind Ruth, the Yankees developed the greatest 1–2 punch that baseball has ever known. The two of them paced the Yanks to another pennant in 1926. The World Series, though, was a different matter.

30. End of a Drought

Until 1926, the St. Louis Cardinals had never won a pennant. They weren't expected to win one in 1926 either. But they did.

There were a number of reasons why the Cards were able to take the flag. First, Branch Rickey's chain-store methods began to show results. Secondly, Rogers Hornsby became playing manager of the club.

Hornsby showed that he was as good a manager as player. Like John McGraw he ruled his club with an iron hand. Hornsby did not have an overpowering ball club, but he squeezed every bit of ability from his players. In addition, he made two trades that helped the Cardinals immensely.

One involved Billy Southworth of the Giants. While Southworth seemed just an average ball player under McGraw, he blossomed into a star when switched to the Cardinals.

Hornsby also snatched up Grover Cleveland Alexander, when the Chicago Cubs put the aging pitcher on the waiver list.

Alexander had been in baseball since 1909 and in the big leagues since 1911. In each of six of his first seven years, he won 22 games or more. On three occasions, while pitching for Philadelphia, he won 30 games. Traded to the Cubs, he continued to be a big winner until 1924. By that time the Cubs—like almost everyone else in baseball—were sure Alexander had come to the end of the road.

The Yankees took three of the first five World Series games in 1926. Babe Ruth, as usual, led the attack. In the fourth game he set a Series record by hitting three home runs.

Although the Cardinals trailed, Hornsby showed his faith in Alexander by calling on him to hurl the sixth game. The old pitcher responded beautifully. The Cards won, tying the Series at three-all. Billy Southworth was a big help to Alexander. He collected a double and a triple. At one point, with two Yankees on base, he made a diving, head-first catch of a sizzling line drive.

After the game, Alexander celebrated, certain he wouldn't be called to duty in the final game. Hornsby, however, decided to have him in the bullpen "just in case."

The Cards were leading the Yanks by a slim margin in the seventh inning of the seventh game, and it looked as if St. Louis would win its first World Championship. Then suddenly pitcher Jess Haines seemed to lose all control of the ball. After getting two strikes on Lou Gehrig, he floated four bad pitches to the plate. Then two more Yankees walked.

"Time out!" Hornsby yelled at the umpires.

Hornsby and the rest of the Cardinal infield gathered around Haines and quickly discovered what was wrong. Haines had thrown so many knuckle balls he had injured the index finger of his pitching hand.

"We'll have to make a change," Hornsby said grimly, for he knew that

85

one of the Yankees' toughest hitters—
Tony Lazzeri—was waiting at the plate.

As Haines took off his glove and moved
dejectedly toward the Cardinal dugout, Hornsby, to everyone's amazement,
waved in Grover Alexander.

The aging pitcher shuffled slowly out
onto the playing field. His cap was
perched on one side of his head, and his
jaws moved slowly over a cud of tobacco.
Every eye in the ball park turned toward
him.

To the fans, Alexander seemed dazed.
Actually he was thinking carefully about
the situation he faced—the inning, the
score, and the batter.

As the fans buzzed, a worried Hornsby
trotted out to meet his pitcher. Later,
Hornsby reported that he knew Alexander was all right as soon as he got a
good look at him.

Methodically Alexander took his warm-
up tosses. Then he faced Lazzeri. The
first pitch was low. "Ball one!" The second was a strike. On the next pitch,
Lazzeri swung. Crack! The ball whizzed
into the left-field seats.

"Foul ball!" cried the umpire. It was
foul, but just by inches. Alexander and
every Cardinal rooter and player in the
park sighed in relief.

The pitcher fussed about the mound
a bit, looked at his catcher's sign, then
fired again.

"Strike thu-ree!"

The ball park rocked with cheers. The
Cardinal bench teemed with excitement.
But Alexander moved to a quiet corner
of the dugout, ignoring everyone.

When a worried teammate questioned
him, Alexander said:

*In the seventh inning of the seventh 1926
Series game, Cardinal pitcher Grover Cleveland Alexander (above) faced one of the
Yankees' toughest hitters, Tony Lazzeri (below).*

86

"Oh, I'm all right. I was just thinking that if I get the side out in the eighth, I'll have a chance to strike Ruth out for the final out."

Alexander set the Yankees down in order in the eighth inning. He also got the first two men out in the ninth. Then Babe Ruth stepped to the plate. By that time he had collected *four* home runs. He had also broken 10 World Series records.

As every fan knew, Ruth could change the whole complexion of the game with one swish of his bat. Naturally Alexander pitched slowly and carefully.

Ball one. Strike one. Ball two. Strike two. Ball three.

Alexander wound and fired the full-count pitch.

"Ball four!" the umpire roared as Alexander missed the corner of the plate. The great Ruth trotted to first base. On Alexander's next pitch, he broke for second. The catcher fired to Hornsby. An umpire's hand shot skyward. His "Yer out!" call was drowned in the roar of the crowd.

The Series was over. The Cardinals became World Champions for the first time in baseball history.

31. The Mightiest Team of All

It's easy to start an argument among ball fans. All you need do, for example, is tell a Giant follower that Connie Mack was a far better manager than John McGraw. Or that Mickey Mantle can run rings around Willie Mays.

You can get some mighty sharp retorts, too, when trying to name the greatest ball team of all time. Unless, that is, you happen to name the New York Yankees of 1927. For this was a team that had everything—speed, crushing power, and a marvelous defense.

The 1927 Yankees started the season in first place—and finished in first place. The winning margin? Nineteen games. The number of victories? One hundred and ten, at that time an American League record.

Babe Ruth, prodded to tremendous efforts by Lou Gehrig, the rookie at first base, stirred fans as never before. For that was the year the home-run king smashed out a total of 60 home runs. Only a few have come close to that record in a 154-game season.

With but one month of the season left, the Bambino had already lofted the ball out of the park 43 times. During that last month—with every fan in the nation watching the results and wondering just how far the big fellow could go—he hit 17, a little better than one every two days.

With two days left, the Babe's total was 57. On the next to last day, he hit two more. Number 60 was blasted into the seats during the final game of the season. The drive itself had a touch of drama. It landed in fair ground by no more than a foot!

Gehrig hit an additional 47 homers, 13 short of Ruth's total. He drove in 174 runs to Ruth's 164, however, while his batting average was .373 to Ruth's .356. He also led the League in doubles.

But Ruth and Gehrig didn't do all the hitting for the Yankees. Center fielder Earle Combs batted .356 and led the League in singles. Left fielder Bob Meusel batted .336. Second baseman Tony Lazzeri pounded out 18 homers and batted .309.

So fearsome was the hitting of this group that it became known as "Murderer's Row." Only one pitcher, Bob Grove of the Athletics, was able to hold the Yankees scoreless in 1927. In a tingling ball game, the A's won 1–0.

Baseball teams do not win pennants without good pitching. The Yankees of 1927 certainly had their share of it. Pitcher Waite Hoyt won 22 games, while losing 7. Herb Pennock won another 19. Much of the credit for the performance of the mound staff, however, went to a relief pitcher—Wilcy "Cy" Moore. This "fireman" appeared in 50 games. He won 19 and lost but 7.

Despite this great performance, the baseball experts felt the Yankees would have trouble in the 1927 World Series. Their opponents were the Pittsburgh Pirates, paced by Paul Waner and Pie Traynor. (Waner hit .380, the best in the National League, while Traynor drove in 124 runs.)

The Pittsburgh club had never fielded a better team.

Before the Series opened in Pittsburgh, both teams worked out in Forbes Field. The Bucs were on the diamond first. Then they dressed and sat in the stands to watch the Yanks, a team most of them had never seen.

To the astonishment and awe of the Pirates, the Yanks seemed to hit only homers during batting practice. The Pirates didn't know it, but sly Miller Huggins had ordered his pitchers to lay the ball in the strike zone without much speed.

Despite a popular legend, the batting practice bombardment didn't faze the Bucs. They fought hard against the Yankees.

The Yanks won the first game 5–4, but three runs were unearned. Ruth failed to hit a homer, although Gehrig hit a triple.

In the second game, the Yanks won 6–2, but the big gun—Babe Ruth—was almost silent in the 11-hit attack.

Unfortunately for the Pirates, Herb Pennock was at his best in the third game at Yankee Stadium. He retired the first 22 batters to face him. It was still a close ball game, though, until the seventh inning. Finally Ruth broke loose, rocketing a drive into the seats with two on base, thereby topping a six-run rally. The final score: Yankees 8, Pittsburgh 1.

The Pirates fought gamely in the fourth contest to prevent a sweep of the Series. Early in the game, Ruth singled one run home. In the fifth inning, he hit a homer with one on base, giving the Yanks a 3 to 0 lead. But the Pirates stormed back in the seventh to tie the score.

The Babe is congratulated by Lou Gehrig at home plate after smashing out his sixtieth homer.

The New York Yankees of 1927. (Bottom row left to right) Ruether, Dugan, Paschal, Ben-gough, Thomas, Gazella, Morehart, and Eddie Bennett, mascot. (Middle row) Shawkey, Giard, Grabowski, O'Leary, Manager Huggins, Fletcher, Pennock, Wera, Collins. (Top row) Gehrig, Meusel, Ruth, Moore, Pipgras, Combs, Miller, Hoyt, Lazzeri, Koenig, Shocker, Durst, and Doc Woods, trainer.

With the score still tied in the bottom of the ninth, the Yankees quickly loaded the bases. But Pirate pitcher John Miljus struck out Gehrig, then Meusel. A wild pitch to the next batter, however, struck the catcher on the knee and bounded into the infield. The break let in the winning run and gave the New York team its second World Series championship.

The Yankees were almost as impressive in 1928. Again they won the pennant, with Ruth hitting 54 homers. And again they crushed the opposition—the St. Louis Cardinals—in the World Series by taking the first four games. Ruth was superb. He gathered 10 hits in 16 appearances for a .625 average. Three of his hits were homers.

It's hard to believe there was ever a better baseball team than the Yankees of 1927 and 1928.

32. Revival in Philadelphia

Was Connie Mack through as a manager? Had he lost his great ability to judge talent and pilot winners? There were many who thought so when the season started in 1929. After all, the Athletics hadn't won a pennant since 1914.

Mack, of course, heard the grumbling, but he paid no attention. As the New York Yankees went roaring through the American League, he slowly rebuilt his once powerful Philadelphia team. He dipped into the Pacific Coast League to sign black-haired, big-eared Mickey Cochrane, a catcher batting .331. He went to Milwaukee and landed Al Simmons, an outfielder batting .398. His old third baseman, Home Run Baker, brought him a 17-year-old giant named Jimmy Foxx. He also brought Robert Moses "Lefty" Grove from Baltimore for $100,000 after the big pitcher had struck out 1,020 batters over a four-year period. The four were not polished performers

when they arrived in Philadelphia, but each had the mark of greatness. They developed rapidly. To this day, Mickey Cochrane is rated as one of the best catchers baseball ever produced. As a slugger, Jimmy Foxx ranks second only to Babe Ruth. Al Simmons knew no peer whenever he stood at the plate with runners on base. As for Grove, he led the American League four times and is one of 13 pitchers who won 300 or more games in the majors.

With this quartet as the nucleus of his ball club, Mack rode to a sixth pennant in 1929. His National League opponent for the World Championship was a soft-spoken, black-eyed Irishman of few words—Joe McCarthy, pilot of the Chicago Cubs.

McCarthy, Mack knew, was a smart manager. He had taken over the Cubs in 1926, after they had spent a season at the bottom of the League. And he had

Catcher Mickey Cochrane (above) and pitcher Lefty Grove (below) were two of the Athletics' stars who helped bring about a "revival in Philadelphia." (In 1934 Grove moved to Boston.)

forged the team into a pennant winner. In his lineup he had the powerful bats of Rogers Hornsby (formerly of the Cardinals), Hack Wilson, and a tomato-faced catcher affectionately known as "Gabby" Hartnett.

Before the season ended, it became fairly obvious that the Cubs and A's would win the flag in their respective leagues. So Mack planned his strategy long before the World Series opener. He revealed these plans to but one man—pitcher Howard Ehmke. To Ehmke's utter surprise, Mack told him:

"Howard, you're going to pitch the first game against the Cubs for me."

"But the season won't be over for another week, or more," Ehmke commented.

"I know," Mack said. "But while we're making our last western trip, the Cubs will be playing New York and Philadelphia on their eastern swing. I want you to stay behind and scout them."

And that's what Ehmke did.

When the first day of the World Series arrived, Ehmke's name was announced as the A's starter. Against him was the Cubs' tough Charlie Root. Groans of disbelief rolled through the Philadelphia rooters.

"Is Mack daft?" some asked. "Why Ehmke's an old man. He's won only seven games all season. Why doesn't Mack start Grove or Earnshaw?"

But Mack wasn't daft, as Ehmke proved. The aging pitcher held the Cubs scoreless until the ninth inning when a run came in on a two-base error. It didn't matter, though, for young Jimmy Foxx had cracked the ball into the

On the first day of the 1929 Series, pitcher Howard Ehmke's name was announced as starter for the Athletics.

bleachers for a run in the seventh inning, while his mates added two more in the ninth. The A's won 3–1. And Ehmke established a new World Series record by striking out 13.

After that stirring start, the A's were almost invincible. They won the series in five games, handing Mack his fourth World Championship, one more than John McGraw's and Miller Huggins' teams had won.

In 1929 the United States began to feel the pinch of the worst depression in its history. Like the rest of the entertainment business, baseball was hard hit.

The worried owners decided that the fans were staying away from the parks because they were tired of seeing so many home runs. So they deadened the ball to encourage the hit-and-run, steal, and bunt techniques.

This change didn't bother the Athletics. In 1930 they won their second straight pennant and whipped the up-and-coming St. Louis Cardinals in six games of World Series play.

The following year Lefty Grove, the dour, hard-bitten mountaineer, had his best season with 31 victories and 4 losses. The Athletics won their third consecutive pennant. The Cardinals, too, won the pennant in 1931. But because of one man, the World Series did not end as it had the year before.

33. Pepper

The St. Louis Cardinals had a talented outfielder-infielder who seemed to have the combined spirit and fire of John McGraw, Hughie Jennings, and Ty Cobb. His name was John "Pepper" Martin.

Frolicsome and happy-go-lucky, Martin enjoyed playing practical jokes on people almost as much as he loved playing baseball. He was especially fond of handing out loaded cigars and cigarettes. Once he leaned out of a hotel window and dropped a paper bag filled with water on the head of his manager.

The enraged manager raced through the hotel until he caught Martin.

"It slipped, honest," Martin grinned.

"If you'll forgive me, I'll hit a homer in the next game."

The manager gave Martin a shake and let him go. The next day the third baseman kept his promise. His home run won the ball game.

Although Martin was a good ball player, few believed he would have more than a routine role in the 1931 World Series against the Athletics. During the first game, Martin got three hits off Lefty Grove, but the A's won anyhow. So the fans were unaware of what was in store for them. In the second game, however, they began to get an inkling of the surprises awaiting them.

In his first time at bat, Martin singled. As the Philadelphia oufielder bobbled the ball momentarily, Martin flew to second and dived into the bag. The outfielder's throw arrived at about the same time. Martin, however, was safe by a whisker.

The fans had barely settled back in their seats when Martin did what many considered impossible. He stole third against Mickey Cochrane! A fly ball then brought him home.

John "Pepper" Martin

In the seventh inning, Martin singled a second time. To show that his first theft of second base wasn't just luck, he promptly swiped the keystone sack again. When the next batter hit the ball to the shortstop, Martin broke all the rules of good base running by racing to third.

As the pitcher wound up and fired to the next hitter Martin was off for the plate. At the last instant, the batter bunted the ball. The squeeze play worked beautifully and Martin slid home with the second run of the game.

St. Louis won that second game and tied the Series. In the important third game, Martin put on another show. In the second inning, he singled a man to third, then went to third on a hit-and-run play, and scored on a fly ball.

In the fourth inning, with a man on first, Martin bought the crowd roaring to its feet when he hit a drive to the top of the right-field scoreboard. A few feet more and the ball would have cleared the wall for a homer. Instead, it dropped to the field. Martin was held to a double, while his teammate stopped at third. Another hit drove in both runs and the Cards went on to win 5–2. This gave them a 2 to 1 lead in the Series.

The Athletics, with veteran George Earnshaw on the mound, won the fourth game 3–0, tying the Series again. Earnshaw seemed able to get everyone out— everyone but Martin. The amazing Cardinal third sacker got two hits and rattled Cochrane again by stealing still another base.

Martin rose to even greater heights in the fifth game. With three hits—one of them a homer—he drove in four of the Cardinals' five runs.

St. Louis lost the sixth game, but won the deciding seventh. Appropriately Martin made a sparkling, one-hand catch for the last out.

Rarely has one man put on such a show in a World Series.

34. The "Called" Shot

Was Babe Ruth a miracle man? Could he call on some superhuman power and hit a homer whenever it was especially important?

Many would dismiss these questions as being too ridiculous to consider. Others are not so sure. They are thinking, no doubt, of Ruth's role in the 1932 World Series.

That season the Babe's home-run production had dropped to 41. But he batted a respectable .341 and drove in 137 runs. Johnny Allen was the Yanks' leading pitcher with 17 victories and 4 losses. As a team, the Yankees were as potent as ever, winning 107 games.

The National League winner was the Chicago Cubs, a team that boasted a new pitching star, Lon Warneke.

The Series opened in New York, and the Yanks promptly won the first two games. By the time the teams arrived in Chicago for the third game, the Cub players were in a bitter frame of mind. They were determined that the Yanks should not repeat their World Series sweeps of 1927 and 1928.

The fans were not so sure. During batting practice Ruth and Gehrig put on an amazing show, pounding 16 homers into the temporary bleachers in deepest center field. Ruth's first blow soared so far and high it almost left the park.

"Each time the ball dropped into the densely packed stands, the crowd gasped," wrote one newspaper reporter. "The spectacle could not have been very heartening to the Cubs."

In the very first inning, Ruth proved his mighty bat was as potent during the game as it was in batting practice. To begin with, the Yanks' Earle Combs had driven a ball right at shortstop Billy Jurges. Jurges, instead of getting an easy out, fired the ball over first baseman Charlie Grimm's head and Combs went to second. This upset pitcher Charley Root, who walked the next man.

Babe Ruth then came to bat. The Cub fans hurled bright yellow lemons at the round-faced slugger, all the while hooting derisively. At the same time, every man in the Cub dugout was on his feet shouting abuse at the Bambino. (The New York *Herald Tribune* later reported that Ruth "paused to jest with the raging Cubs, pointed to the right field bleachers, and grinned.")

Root's first two pitches were wide. Ruth knew the Chicago hurler would

Charlie Root, the man who pitched Ruth's famous "called" shot.

have to get the next one in the strike zone, or risk loading the bases for the next hitter—Lou Gehrig. When the pitch came, Ruth was ready.

"Crack!"

Just as in batting practice, the ball spun over the fence and into the bleachers. The Yanks led 3–0.

The crowd got back at Ruth in the fourth inning when the Cubs were at bat. By that time the score was 4–3, still in favor of the Yanks. Billy Jurges drove a low liner toward Ruth, who raced in

and made an attempt to catch the ball at his shoe tops. He missed. Jurges rounded first and sped on. Although Ruth made a fine recovery of the ball and a powerful, accurate throw, Jurges slid into second safely, beating the tag by an eyelash. The Chicago supporters were wild with glee.

Again Ruth seemed to enjoy the storm. He smilingly raised his cap and waved it at the stands. A few minutes later, the fans had another go at him as Tony Lazzeri made an error that enabled Jurges to score the tying run.

The whooping rose to a deafening crescendo in the top of the fifth, for Ruth was the first batter up for the Yankees. As he strode smilingly to the plate, his powerful arms swung three bats from one shoulder to another. He threw two bats to the bat boy and moved into the batter's box. At that moment, a single lemon, glinting brightly in the sunlight, bounded and rolled toward his feet.

With that taunting note, the stage was set for one of the most talked-about scenes in all baseball history.

". . . in no mistaken motion," the New York *Times* later reported, "the Babe notified the crowd that the nature of his retaliation would be a wallop right out of the confines of the park."

The crowd and the Cub bench, apparently galled by Ruth's audacity, heaped new abuse on the Yankee outfielder. Never had such wild-eyed partisanship been witnessed at a World Series.

Charlie Root took his windup, kicked, and whipped the ball past Ruth's knees for a called strike. The shriek of the Chi-

95

cago rooters hit another high.

Ruth, undisturbed, raised one finger. Grinning broadly, he bobbed his head and waved his hand to the Cub bench and each section of the park. Root pitched again. This time it was "Ball one!"

Ruth, still smiling broadly, again made the appropriate sign with his fingers—one-and-one.

Root kept pitching. The count rose to two-and-two while Ruth continued his pantomime. With each gesture the fans roared anew; some with applause, some with derision.

Root made his fifth pitch. Here's the way a *Times* man described what happened in that memorable moment:

"Then the mightiest blow of all fell. It was a tremendous smash that bore straight over the center in an enormous arc, came down alongside the flagpole and disappeared.

"The crowd, unmindful of anything except that it had just witnessed an epic feat, let loose with a great salvo of applause."

Brought to its feet by Ruth's powerful drive, the crowd had barely settled back when Lou Gehrig lashed another homer to the same spot to drive Charlie Root from the game.

"It was like a flash of lightning and a clap of thunder," a newsman wrote.

The savage blows by Ruth and Gehrig fashioned another victory for the Yankees. In the clubhouse after the game, Ruth modestly brushed aside the praise.

"Shucks, that big wind blowing toward the outfield helped me a lot," he said.

Ruth's home run in the fifth inning of the 1932 World Series has probably created more discussion than any other single play in baseball. Many fans stated that when Ruth raised his hand between the deliveries offered by Root he was telling everybody he intended to blast the ball into the bleachers. In other words, he was "calling the shot."

Root, among others, said Babe did no such thing. He was putting up his finger simply to indicate the count.

For years several writers who attended the game tried to prove that Ruth actually put the ball where he wanted it in the 1932 Series.

Only Ruth really knew.

The big black number "3" meant just one thing to Yankee fans during the 1920s—Babe Ruth.

35. The Loud One

Jay Hanna Dean was a friendly, loud-talking pitcher who made extraordinary claims about what he could do, then went ahead and proved he could do them.

The St. Louis Cardinals signed "Dizzy" Dean in 1929, after he had served a hitch in the Army.

Assigned to St. Joseph of the Western Association, Dean won 17 games in his first season of professional ball. Promoted to Houston of the Texas League, Dean won 26 games.

The next stop, of course, was the parent team, the St. Louis Cardinals. Dean's blazing fast ball and crackling curve enabled him to lead the League in strikeouts four years in a row. And during that period the powerful right-hander struck out more than 200 batters a season.

By the spring of 1934 there were two Deans on the Cardinal roster—Dizzy and his brother, Paul Dean, who later was nicknamed "Daffy."

Although the Cards had finished fifth in 1933, Dizzy freely predicted the Red Birds would easily win the flag in 1934.

"Why, me and Paul will win 40 or 45 games between us," Dizzy said. "If all those other pitchers win mebbe 50 more we'll be in."

The Loud One, surprisingly enough, was too modest in his forecast. The Deans won 49 games.

It wasn't easy, of course. The Dean boys caused all sorts of trouble. After losing a double-header against the Chicago Cubs, the Deans deliberately missed a train for Detroit, where the Cardinals were to play the Tigers in an exhibition game. The Cards' new manager, Frank Frisch, promptly slapped a healthy fine on the brothers. Dizzy and Daffy were so enraged they tore up their uniforms. As a matter of fact, they tore them up twice. There weren't any newspaper photographers around to take pictures the first time.

The rest of Frankie Frisch's "Gas House Gang," as the rough-and-tumble Cardinals were called, stood by their manager. So did Commissioner Kenesaw Mountain Landis.

When the Deans saw that they were standing alone, they decided to behave. Their decision was a good thing for the Cards—and for baseball. For the Deans not only won ball games, they also drew fans.

After the Detroit incident, the St. Louis Cardinals won seven in a row and moved into contention for the flag.

It was a tough fight, though. On June 8, 1934, the Giants were in first place. They were still there on September 7, with the Cardinals trailing by seven games. Gradually, however, the Giants lost their lead. On the last day of the season, the Cards were playing Cincinnati while the Giants were host to the Dodgers. The Cards were leading the Giants by one game.

In the ninth inning of their game with the Cincinnati Reds, the Cardinals were ahead 9–0. Dean was on the way to his

The antics of the Dean brothers won them the nicknames of Dizzy (left) and Daffy. Here they are shown in a more sober moment.

99

thirtieth victory and seventh shutout of the season—the best record in the League. But the pesky Reds suddenly turned on Dean. A single, double, and walk filled the bases with none out.

At this precise moment a message was flashed to the ball park from New York. It read: "Dodgers 8, Giants 5."

A big grin spread across Dizzy's amiable face. He promptly struck out the next two hitters. The third one popped up to the catcher. The Cardinals were National League champions.

The Deans were such an attraction that newspapers often ran headlines like DEANS VS GIANTS TODAY.

The Detroit Tigers had slipped badly after the heyday of their biggest star, Ty Cobb. But Mickey Cochrane, purchased from the Athletics, became manager of the Tigers. And in 1934 he led them to the capture of the American League pennant. Cochrane was blessed with a fine pitching staff that year. A big righthander, Lynwood Thomas Rowe, was the anchor man of the staff. He won 24 games, while losing only 8. Rowe, familiarly known as "Schoolboy," won 16 of the games in a row.

Tommy Bridges added 22 victories to Rowe's 24 and Eldon Auker won another 15.

Along with good pitching, the Tigers had good hitting—especially from their young first baseman, Henry Benjamin Greenberg. Greenberg, a dedicated player who took his work very seriously, went on to become one of the great batting stars of the game. (Once during his career, he hit nothing but home runs

Pitcher Lynwood "Schoolboy" Rowe (above) and first baseman Hank Greenberg (below) helped the Tigers win the 1934 pennant.

100

every time he came to bat in nine consecutive games.)

By the opening of the 1934 World Series, Dizzy Dean was telling all who would listen that he and Paul should pitch all the games.

"After all, we won the pennant and we should get the chance to win the Series," Dean said.

The Cardinals won the Series in seven games. Dizzy and Daffy were not allowed to pitch all seven, but they each won two.

Schoolboy Rowe turned in one of the best World Series performances of all time when he retired 22 St. Louis batters in a row in the second game. He made history of another sort when he said a few words to a radio audience, a novelty at that time.

"How'm I doin', Edna?" he said happily. It was a question intended for his fiancée.

After that the brash Cardinals constantly uttered the cry every time Rowe moved about the diamond.

"How'm I doin', Edna? How'm I doin', Edna?" Small wonder that the Cardinals won the final game by a score of 11–0.

36. The Lean One

Most pitchers make a baseball curve by rotating the throwing hand and wrist outward at the end of the delivery. But Carl Owen Hubbell, a left-hander, made a specialty of turning his pitching hand inward as he let go of the ball. This gave him a curving pitch called a "screwball." While the pitch was not entirely new, Hubbell put it to use as never before.

Hubbell had come out of the Texas League to join the Giants in 1928. By the time he left the majors, he had won a total of 253 games. He enjoyed many other distinctions. One season, for example, he pitched 10 shutouts. He also hurled 46 consecutive scoreless innings. He was so reliable a pitcher that the Giants dubbed him "The Meal Ticket."

Hubbell had a long and distinguished career, but he is remembered most for a performance that took place in the Polo Grounds in 1934 before some 50,000 fans. It happened during the first three innings of the second All-Star game.

The tradition of the All-Star game had been introduced in 1933. Arch Ward, sports editor of the Chicago *Tribune*, suggested that a game between the best players of each major league would help build up attendance. It had been slipping badly. Ward also thought the first All-Star game should be played in Chicago, because the World's Fair was opening there that year.

John McGraw, who had recently resigned as manager of the Giants, was selected to manage the National League squad. The leader of the American League team was the ageless Connie Mack. A homer by Babe Ruth paced the

By consecutively striking out five of baseball's most powerful hitters, Carl Hubbell became the talk of the baseball world.

American League to a 4–2 victory.

The second All-Star game was held in New York City in 1934. Just before the start of the game Carl Hubbell was presented with an award naming him as the outstanding National League player of the previous year. But Hubbell didn't look very outstanding as he began his three-inning stint. The first man up, Charlie Gehringer, singled. When outfielder Wally Berger juggled the ball, Gehringer flew to second, sliding safely to the bag just ahead of Berger's throw.

Hubbell, somewhat flustered, then did an unusual thing. He walked the next batter, Heinie Manush. That put two men on base with none out.

The next batter? It was a familiar figure in a Yankee uniform. A big, black Number 3 on back of the player's shirt spelled out his name to all: Babe Ruth.

Hubbell, working slowly and deliberately, went to his "stretch" position, glanced at the runners on first and second, then fired at the plate.

"Ball one!" the umpire yelled.

Hubbell tightened his belt, tugged his cap, and pitched again.

"Strike one!" the umpire tolled, as Ruth watched Hubbell's second pitch go by. The count went on:

"Strike two!"

"Strike thu-reee!"

The Babe turned and walked to the bench. He hadn't even attempted a swing.

Hubbell had a long way to go, though. Behind Ruth was Lou Gehrig. Then Jimmy Foxx, Al Simmons, and Joe Cronin.

Hubbell, seemingly the calmest person in the park, threw Gehrig a ball on the first pitch. He threw three more pitches. All were strikes. Gehringer and Manush worked a double steal as the last pitch whizzed by Gehrig.

Jimmy Foxx came to the plate. A sin-

Jimmy Foxx (left) and Joe Cronin, two of the great hitters struck out by Hubbell in the 1934 All-Star game.

gle would mean two runs. Hubbell remained calm. His first pitch was a strike.

Hubbell glanced at the runner on third, wound up and delivered his second pitch to Foxx. The Athletic slugger took a vicious cut at the ball, but fouled it off. It was strike two.

Carl Hubbell then cut loose with his famous screwball. Foxx went down swinging. The inning was over.

Frank Frisch was the first man up for the National Leaguers. He got his team off to a fast start by banging a homer off the pitch of Vernon "Lefty" Gomez. But Gomez then struck out the next three hitters.

The spotlight swung back to Hubbell. He took up where he had left off in the previous inning. He struck out Al Simmons and Joe Cronin. Bill Dickey, however, made a single, bringing Gomez to

bat. Hubbell threw one pitch. It was a strike. He threw another. Another strike. In swinging at the ball, Gomez' bat slipped from his hand and flew toward second base.

"Leave it there," Frisch yelled at Gomez. "You won't need it."

He was right. Hubbell struck Gomez out on the next pitch.

That finished Hubbell's share of the mound chores. Although the American League eventually won the ball game, Hubbell was the talk of the baseball world. After all, he had consecutively struck out five of baseball's most powerful hitters. And of the fifteen strikes he pitched past these batters, only one—the foul by Foxx—was touched by a bat.

"Unquestionably, it was the greatest pitching performance I have ever seen," Joe Cronin said after the ball game. Few would dispute Cronin's view.

37. From Daylight to Dark

Because of the Great Depression, Americans watched their pocketbooks very carefully in the mid-thirties. Baseball suffered and the club owners looked for ways to bolster the gate receipts. One man in particular favored a new idea— night baseball.

Larry MacPhail was a brilliant, red-haired promoter with a quick temper. He had been hired by a Cincinnati bank to get the ailing Cincinnati Reds on the profit side of the ledger. His proposal to

play baseball under a set of lights horrified both leagues. It also made some of the fans unhappy.

The idea, of course, was not original with MacPhail. Sports contests under lights had been attempted as early as the 1800s. But the lighting equipment was very poor, and the early experiments failed.

Since that time, however, the equipment had improved immensely. So much so that the minor leagues had begun to play night games in 1930. In no time, the minors tripled gate attendance.

"At least let us give it a try," MacPhail argued.

Finally the National League agreed. In 1935 the Reds planned seven home games under lights.

MacPhail, always a great showman, staged a fireworks display before the first of the night games. He also cleverly arranged for the President of the United States, Franklin D. Roosevelt, to turn on the lights. The President did this by pressing a button in his office at the White House.

Although the Cincinnati players were enthusiastic about defeating the Philadelphia Phillies that night, they had mixed feelings about playing after dark. Opinion seemed to be divided among the fans, too.

Gradually, however, MacPhail's idea took hold and night baseball became a great success.

38. The Babe Bows Out

Like the Cincinnati Reds, the Boston Braves were also seeking ways to bring fans to their ball park in 1935. Instead of introducing night ball, though, the Braves simply hired the biggest attraction baseball had ever known—Babe Ruth.

The Braves did it in a big way, too. They made Babe a vice-president—the only vice-president who ever played right field.

Although Ruth appeared in but 28 games, he got the usual thundering ovation whenever he moved across the diamond. Of the thirteen hits Babe recorded that year, six were homers.

Three of his homers were among the most memorable of all. He hit them in a game against the Pirates at Forbes Field. And each one had the true Ruthian touch—high, booming arcs that made the fans gasp. One cleared the right-field roof at Forbes Field, which has rarely been done. That last homer was number 714, a record that stands alone by a wide margin.

But the Babe didn't like being a vaudeville attraction. He was a ball player. And if he couldn't play every day he didn't want to play at all. The season was less than half over when he quietly left the Braves. He was 40 at the time.

Although Babe was ignored for the next three years, he wasn't quite through with baseball. In 1938 he walked into Ebbets Field to watch the Brooklyn Dodgers play. As Ruth's well-known camel-hair cap bobbed along the aisles, the crowd began to murmur. The murmur grew and grew until it was a full-throated roar.

"It's the Babe!" "It's the Babe!" the fans shouted gleefully as they strained to catch a glimpse of the famous player.

The Babe poses for news photographers on Babe Ruth Day at Yankee Stadium.

The Dodger management got the message fast: there was still magic in the name of Babe Ruth. They hired the Bambino the next day as a batting instructor. It was understood that he would be considered for the manager's job the next year. Although the Dodgers finished seventh, they did very well at the gate. But the Dodgers and the Babe parted company at the end of the season.

The Babe then sought the one thing he wanted most—to manage the New York Yankees. The chance never came. It almost broke his heart.

In August of 1942 he agreed to appear at a benefit game in Yankee Stadium. A smart publicist had dreamed up the idea of having Walter Johnson pitch to the once mighty Ruth during a double-header intermission.

Ruth was 47 at the time, Johnson 55. Ruth hadn't touched a bat in four years, while Johnson hadn't thrown a ball in three. Could Johnson get the ball over the plate? Could Ruth hit it if he did?

Two days before the exhibition Ruth showed he still had some of the old touch. After battling his way through a swarm of youngsters, he took batting practice with the Yanks. With little difficulty he pounded the ball into the seats several times.

On the day Ruth was to face Johnson, the Yankee ball park was opened at 8:30 A.M. By noon more than 69,000 fans filled all available space. And when the first game was over, there was little doubt as to why they had come.

"We want Babe!" "We want Babe!" "We want Babe!" they chanted over and over.

Soon Johnson was taking his famous windup. Ruth, his oval face beaming, stood at the plate as always—feet together, head cocked sideways, bat twitching.

The first pitch by Johnson was a ball. The second a called strike. The third another ball. Then, *bang!* The ball flew into the right-field bleachers for a homer.

"Atta boy, Babe!" the crowd yelled.

Johnson made 15 more pitches. Out of that assortment, Ruth hit a single, high fly, and just missed putting the ball into the bleachers in deepest center field, which would have been a spectacular shot. On the last pitch, Babe powdered the ball deep into the right-field stands. Although it was foul by a few inches, Ruth trotted around the bases, doffing his cap as he went. As he crossed the plate, a grinning Johnson gripped his hand warmly. And after one last, lingering look around the great stadium, Ruth ducked into the dugout and disappeared. The crowd called and called for him to return, but he never did.

It was Ruth's last big scene.

39. The Rookies

Only a few of the hundreds of young men who break into professional baseball each year ever become stars. During the thirties and forties there were four, however, who were so outstanding they will be remembered by ball fans as long as baseball exists.

One of these is the quiet, long-legged Californian who almost replaced Babe Ruth in the hearts of Yankee rooters. His name is Joseph DiMaggio.

Strangely enough, Joe DiMaggio wasn't much interested in baseball as a youngster. He favored tennis. And when he left high school, he went to work to help the family.

But Joe's brothers—Vincent and Dominic—were baseball-minded, and both eventually made their way into the major leagues. They urged young Joe to attend a school for baseball prospects in San Francisco early in the thirties. Spotted by a scout, he was signed by the San Francisco Seals as a shortstop, but later was switched to the outfield.

DiMaggio soon set the Pacific Coast League afire. During one period he hit safely at least once in each of 61 consecutive games. In 1935 he batted .398, hit 34 homers, stole 24 bases, and drove in 154 runs.

Although DiMaggio injured his knee in a freak accident, the Yankees gave the Seals $25,000 and five players for the outfielder.

In 1936 DiMaggio opened the season in center field for the Yankees. He was a replacement for Earle Combs, who was out of the lineup with a shoulder injury. DiMaggio started well, banging out three hits, one of them a triple.

A second rookie, Robert Feller, made as remarkable a debut as DiMaggio that same year. Feller went into the big leagues as a pitcher for the Cleveland Indians. In his first league game he struck out 15 St. Louis batsmen.

Bobby Feller was taught baseball by his father, a hard-working Iowa farmer. The elder Feller took time out from his daily chores to have the boy pitch to him as he stood with his back to the side of the barn. By the time Bobby was 10 years old, he could throw a baseball more than 275 feet.

As Bobby Feller grew older, his arm naturally got stronger. The daily workouts ended when a pitch broke through his father's hands, injuring three ribs.

The Cleveland Indians signed Feller when he was 16 years old. Although he couldn't play in official games until he left high school, he often practiced with the Indians during the summer months.

On one occasion he pitched against the St. Louis Cardinals' Gas House Gang in an exhibition game. He whiffed eight of nine batters he faced.

A few years after DiMaggio and Feller appeared in the majors, a tall, gangling youngster arrived at the spring training camp of the Boston Red Sox. He immediately let everyone know he was ready to move into the Boston outfield as a

FOUR ROOKIES WHO MADE GOOD

Joe DiMaggio

Bob Feller

Ted Williams

Stan Musial

starter. His name? Theodore "Ted" Williams.

At first base was old "double XX"—Jimmy Foxx. Foxx twice hit more than 50 homers a season and eventually placed second only to Ruth in total homers, with 534.

"Wait until you see Foxx hit, kid, and you'll think twice about taking this job," one of the Sox players cautioned Williams.

"Wait until Foxx sees *me* hit," Williams replied.

Williams didn't make the parent club that season and was sent to Minneapolis for seasoning. As he left, one of the older players said:

"So long, busher!"

"I'll be back," Williams retorted.

He was true to his word. The next season he rejoined the Red Sox and batted a neat .327. By the time he ended his career in 1960, Williams had compiled one of the most remarkable batting records in the history of the game. And he had earned more money than any other player except Babe Ruth.

The player who ranks next in earnings signed his first professional contract at about the same time Ted Williams began playing for Boston. He was Stan "The Man" Musial.

Stan Musial started as a pitcher-outfielder in the Mountain States League when he was 17 years old. One day while he was playing the outfield he tried to make a shoestring catch of a line drive. He took a tumble, crashing his shoulder into the ground. The accident almost finished him as a ball player, for his arm suddenly went dead. Later that season, the arm came back to life. By that time Stan had convinced his manager that he would be more valuable as an outfielder than as a pitcher. He was batting .369. Promoted to Rochester in the International League, he hit .327. Manager Billy Southworth quickly brought him to the St. Louis Cardinals for the last month of 1941. There Musial pounded the ball for a sensational .426, proving that he was big league material.

In his first full year with the Cards, Stan hit a respectable .315. In his second year he led the National League with .357. Like Williams, he became one of the game's best hitters, winning the National League batting title six more times.

The arrival of DiMaggio, Feller, Williams, and Musial in the majors ushered in a bright new day for baseball and its fans.

40. Yankee Hearts

Although Joe McCarthy was fortunate enough to have a great collection of stars in Yankee flannels in the late thirties, he ran his ball club as a unit.

Some say he developed a machine that operated so efficiently he only had to push a button to win a ball game.

The Yankees, if one looks at the record, certainly did seem to have a machine-like quality. For they won four pennants between 1936 and 1939. And their World Series record of the same period reads as follows:

New York Yankees 4 games, New York Giants 2 games

New York Yankees 4 games, New York Giants 1 game

New York Yankees 4 games, Cincinnati Reds 0

New York Yankees 4 games, Chicago Cubs 0

Four pennants and four World Championships in a row! Only three losses in 19 World Series games played.

But Joe McCarthy was not a "push-button manager," for it takes great skill to handle a large group of talented ball players. It isn't easy to keep them happy and to keep them winning. As for the ball players, they need more than mechanical ability to win consistently. It takes spirit, unselfishness, and courage.

One man above all others proved just how human the Yankees of the late thirties were. He was Lou Gehrig.

In 1936—at the start of the Yanks' winning streak—Gehrig led the American League in home runs with 49. And he batted a sparkling .354. The next year Joe DiMaggio took the title by hitting 46 homers.

By the following season Gehrig's batting average and homer production had dropped considerably. At first Lou and the Yankees weren't too concerned.

"Lou's just had a bad year," was the general opinion.

When the next season began, though, it became clear that something was wrong with Lou. His play was ragged and grew more so as the schedule wore on. For the first time pitchers found it easy to strike him out.

Still Joe McCarthy didn't have the heart to bench the proud slugger.

Finally, on May 2, Lou spoke to his manager.

"Joe, I'm out of the lineup. I'm just not doing the team any good."

It was a painful moment for both men. But neither could deny the truth of Gehrig's words.

That was the day, of course, that Lou Gehrig established his all-time record of having played in 2,130 consecutive games. While he set many other records, it is this rugged performance that will be remembered longest.

But what was wrong with the Iron Horse? He was still a young man. He should have had many playing years left.

Lou set out to find the answer. Doctors discovered he had a rare and dread disease: amytrophic lateral sclerosis. A severe form of polio, it is now called "Gehrig's disease."

His body visibly weakened by his fatal illness, Lou Gehrig (left) chats with his former team-mates in the Yankee locker room.

Right after he took himself out of the lineup, Lou's health worsened rapidly. The Yankees pretended not to notice.

On July 4, 1939, there was a "Lou Gehrig Day" at Yankee Stadium. All the old members of the superb 1927 team were brought together for the occasion. They gathered about Gehrig in the outfield, watching proudly as the 1927 pennant was drawn to the top of the flagpole. Then, along with the crowd, they listened with approval as each of the many dignitaries on the field spoke in glowing terms of their stricken former teammate.

Gehrig stood with head bowed, hands thrust deep into the rear pockets of his uniform pants. Occasionally he scratched the turf with one spiked shoe, then the other.

Suddenly the microphone was thrust at Lou. Hushed thousands waited for him to speak. But the broad-shouldered Yankee only gulped and kept his eyes fastened to the ground.

Joe McCarthy stepped forward quickly, patted Lou on the back, and spoke to him softly. It seemed to many that Joe was saying, as he had during many a tough spot in a ball game, "Come on, boy, you can do it!"

Some say Lou had carefully prepared a speech the night before. If so, he apparently decided against using it. For when he responded to McCarthy's urging and looked at the row upon row of faces that walled the park, he said simply:

"What young man wouldn't give anything to mingle with such men for a single day as I have for all these years?

Manager Joe McCarthy pats "The Iron Man" on the back.

Babe Ruth throws his arms around the big first baseman.

You've been reading about my bad breaks for weeks now. But today I think I'm the luckiest man alive. I now feel more than ever that I have much to live for."

When Gehrig finished speaking, Babe Ruth threw his arms around the big first baseman and hugged him. Gehrig's sincere, humbled words and Ruth's impulsive gesture warmed every heart and brought tears to many pairs of eyes.

There are those who believe Gehrig knew he was dying as he spoke at the Stadium that memorable day. If this is true, his brief speech points up the selflessness and bravery of the man.

Lou turned in his uniform after the World Series. He died less than two years later, but his magnificent playing record lives on.

41. The Daffiness Boys

In Brooklyn people were talking about the Dodgers—but for all the wrong reasons. The ball club that had won pennants in 1916 and 1920 wasn't doing very well.

According to baseball folklore, two Brooklyn fans sat in the bleachers on a sunny summer afternoon. One was anxiously watching the diamond, where the Dodgers had launched a sudden rally against the Giants. The other was working over his scorecard.

"Hey! Look!" shouted the first one, shoving an elbow into his friend's ribs. "The Dodgers have three men on base!"

His friend didn't even look up.

"Yeah?" he asked casually. "Which base?"

Such was the attitude of the large and loyal Brooklyn following in the years between 1920 and 1940. For these were the "Daffiness Days," when anything could happen in Brooklyn—and usually did.

In the twenties Floyd "Babe" Herman

was one of the most erratic of the Brooklyn base runners. Without doubt he can be blamed for inspiring the three-men-on-a-base story recounted above. In 1926 Herman got involved in one of the most confounding plays imaginable. It happened during a double-header played against the Boston Braves at Brooklyn.

Brooklyn's Hank DeBerry was on third, Dazzy Vance was on second, and Chick Fewster was on first when Herman came to bat. Herman, always a wonderful hitter, bashed the ball to right field, where it caromed off the wall. DeBerry scored. Vance moved to third, deciding to take only one base. But Fewster took two bases, arriving at third with Vance. Herman, a little more ambitious than anyone else, took three bases. Suddenly there were three men on third base! They didn't stay there long, however. When Herman slid into third, Fewster jumped over his legs and was called out for passing a base runner. Then, since Vance was the only one entitled to hold third,

The Dodgers' Babe Herman at bat during a practice session.

"Uncle Robbie" displays a trophy—a golf trophy!—for the benefit of his daffy Dodgers.

Herman was declared out when the Braves' third baseman tagged him with the ball. In spite of the incident the Brooklyn team whipped the Braves in both games by scores of 4–2 and 11–3.

On another occasion, Herman drove a ball to the outfield with a runner on first. Herman was sure he had a double. He put his head down, raced to first, and turned for second.

The other runner, however, got as far as second, then realized the ball might be caught. Quick as a flash he spun around and headed back to first. He and Herman passed each other going in *opposite directions!*

Wilbert Robinson was at the Brooklyn helm during a great part of the "Daffiness Days." The old Oriole catcher was so good-humored and easy-going that everyone spoke of him as "Uncle Robbie." And the Brooklyn players, in those days, were called the "Robins" in his honor.

Although the team lolled in sixth place most of the time, it did have a few really good ball players on the roster. Actually Babe Herman himself was a much maligned ball player. He was an excellent hitter, once batting .393 for the Dodgers. And pitcher Dazzy Vance was another fine player. He had joined the team after spending 11 years in the minors. Vance led the League in strikeouts seven seasons in a row. In 10 years with Brooklyn, he whiffed 2,045 batters. One year he struck out 262 while winning 28 games.

As a team, though, Brooklyn was pretty poor. They made a brief comeback in 1930 when for 75 days they held first place in the National League. But by the end of the season they were down to fourth place. Robinson was demoted from president to just plain manager. The next year Brooklyn stayed in fourth place, and Robbie resigned at the end of the season.

The fumbling management tried several cures. They even brought back a one-time Brooklyn player, Casey Stengel, to act as coach and then as team manager. But the Dodgers slipped back to sixth place. Even the loyal fans stopped turning out to watch the "Daffiness Boys."

At the beginning of the 1934 season a sports writer asked Bill Terry, playing manager of the Giants, what he thought about Brooklyn's chances.

"Brooklyn?" Terry snapped. "Are they still in the League?"

Terry was to regret that remark. On the last Saturday of the season the Giants played the Dodgers at the Polo Grounds. Fifty thousand Brooklynites were screaming: "Is Brooklyn still in the league? You'll find out today, you bum."

And Terry did find out—the Dodgers beat the Giants 5–1. The following day they beat them again—8–5. Because of the fierce fight put up by the Dodgers the unfortunate Giants lost the pennant to the Cardinals.

By the beginning of the 1939 season the Dodger management had made really sweeping changes. Larry MacPhail, the man who had brought night baseball to Cincinnati, was the new president of the club. A tough shortstop by the name of Leo Durocher had taken over as manager.

Despite his ability as a fast, loud talker, Leo Durocher fails to change the umpire's decision.

Leo Durocher had started in the majors as an infielder with the New York Yankees. While not a .300 hitter, he was dangerous at the plate with men on base. In the field he was slick and quick.

Durocher talked so fast, so loudly, and so often that sports writers called him "Leo the Lip." His brashness and his talent for picking fights caused the Yankees to send him packing to the National League, where he played with the Reds and Cardinals before joining the Dodgers.

As a manager, Durocher was a throwback to John McGraw. He bullied the umpires and constantly flayed his opponents with his brassy voice and quick tongue. Although his manners were not the best, he knew how to excite his ball club and keep it moving.

By the end of the 1940 season the Dodgers had fought their way to second place in the National League, and they had won 16 out of 21 games with the Giants. From all over Brooklyn came the cry: "Wait till next year!"

And sure enough, 1941 proved to be the year the Dodgers finally won their third pennant. Although they lost the World Series to the Yankees in five games, they made one thing quite clear. The daffiness days were over.

42. The Post-War Comeback

From 1942 through 1945, professional baseball suffered from both lack of players and lack of fans. For these were the years when America was fighting in World War II. As scores of players changed from flannels to khaki and navy blue, the quality of major league baseball dropped very low indeed. And thousands of devoted fans were away fighting on far-flung fronts throughout the world.

With the end of the war, however, the big league stars streamed back to their ball clubs, and the fans turned out as never before.

Despite a long tour of military duty, Ted Williams batted .342 in the 1946 season. He also hit 38 homers, helping the Red Sox to run away with the pennant. In the 1946 All-Star game, Williams put on a show that almost equaled that of Carl Hubbell in 1934. In four turns at bat Williams hit two homers and two singles.

In the National League, the Cardinals and Dodgers fought a day-by-day battle for the pennant. Although the Cards were favored, Leo Durocher had the Dodgers so fired up they played a spectacular brand of ball.

On the last day of the season, the Dodgers played Boston at Ebbets Field, while the Cardinals played the Cubs in Chicago. The teams were tied for first place. The Dodgers lost and so did the Cards.

In the first play-off in National League history, the Cardinals downed Brooklyn in two games in a best-of-three series.

One of the returned Cardinal players was Stan Musial. He won his second batting title with .365. He seemed to have his best days when playing against Brooklyn. The Cardinals also benefitted from good pitching by Murry Dickson and Harry "The Cat" Brecheen. Dickson led the League with a 15-6 record.

In World Series play the Cards were at their best, beating the hard-hitting Red Sox in seven thrilling games. Brecheen won three games and allowed but one earned run in twenty innings.

Two American League pitchers—the Tigers' "Prince" Hal Newhouser and the Indians' Bobby Feller—each won twenty-six games that year. Feller also struck out 348 batters. This broke the record of 343 strike-outs in one season set by the eccentric Rube Waddell 42 years earlier.

Baseball had returned with a new punch!

43. A New Star for the Dodgers

While the major leagues were getting back to normal in 1946, something unusual happened in the International League. On opening day in Jersey City's Roosevelt Stadium a Negro played second base for the Montreal Royals. His name was Jackie Robinson. The 27-year-old, California-born Robinson had been signed to a Royals contract shortly after the 1945 World Series. Until that day Negroes had been kept out of professional baseball because of racial prejudice. The man who dared to sign up Robinson was Branch Rickey, who was now the general manager of the Brooklyn Dodgers. The Dodger organization used the Montreal Royals as a training ground.

Jackie Robinson was a remarkable athlete. He excelled in track, football, and basketball in high school and college. A highly intelligent player, he was also a determined competitor.

Before he finished college, Robinson went into the Army, serving as a 2nd lieutenant. Following that, he began playing baseball with the Kansas City Monarchs, an all-Negro team. It was there that Branch Rickey found him.

In his first game at Roosevelt Stadium, Robinson made it clear he had the potential of a big league star. He hit a homer and two singles, stole two bases, and scored four runs as the Royals won 14 to 1.

By the end of the season, Jackie had won the International League batting title. He also outshone every second baseman in the League in fielding and all-around play. More important, he was

Branch Rickey signs up Jackie Robinson for his second season.

Robinson, a whizz on the base paths, makes it home—minus his hat!

cheered wildly by the fans. And his teammates liked him.

Jackie's success was so spectacular that Branch Rickey had him report to the Dodgers the next season. He played a new position—first base—so that veteran Eddie Stanky could remain at second.

All but a few of the Dodgers accepted Jackie. But players on other teams, notably the Phillies and Cardinals, taunted him unmercifully. At one point the Cardinals threatened to strike if Robinson was in the lineup against them.

But Cardinal owner Sam Breadon quickly put a stop to the threat. Breadon's hand was strengthened by National League President Ford Frick, who said he would suspend anyone who struck over the issue of Robinson's play-

ing, "even if it means wrecking the League.

"This is the United States of America and one player has as much right to play as another," Frick said sternly.

Robinson had promised Rickey that he would ignore the bench jockeying and concentrate on his game. Through great effort he kept his word. It was the right formula, too. For in that first year with the Dodgers, Robinson won the "Rookie of the Year" title and batted .296.

In 1949 Robinson won the batting title, and was named the Most Valuable Player in the National League. He led the League twice in stolen bases and three times in fielding, and became one of the great stars of the game before he retired.

44. The Yanks Again

The Dodgers played the 1947 season under a new manager, Burt Shotton. Shotton was an old-time baseball man, and he led the Brooklyn team to another pennant.

In the American League it was the New York Yankees again. They built a heavy attack around Joe DiMaggio, who won the 1947 Most Valuable Player award in the American League. The Yankees had fine pitching to go with the hitting. Allie Reynolds, for example,

was the best in the majors with an 18-5 record.

The Yankees also developed a remarkable relief pitcher in Joe Page, a happy-go-lucky left-hander who reminded the fans of Dizzy Dean. Like Dean, Page used but one method to snuff out a batting rally. He would rear back and fire the ball toward the plate as hard as he could.

The 1947 World Series was remarkable in many ways. At the gate the Yankees and the Dodgers drew almost 390,-000 fans as the Series went to seven games. But many more thousands "saw" the game, for that year the Bell Telephone System opened the nation's first television network. It linked New York, Philadelphia, Baltimore, and Washington.

The Series itself was full of thrills. Few games, however, matched the fourth for sheer drama. The Yankees, playing in Ebbets Field, were leading in games by 2 to 1. By the bottom of the ninth in the fourth game they were ahead 2 to 1 in score. More important, Yankee pitcher Floyd "Bill" Bevens had a no-hitter going.

Bevens walked outfielder Carl Furillo to put the tying run on base. Burt Shotton replaced Furillo with Al Gionfriddo, another outfielder. Gionfriddo was a small man with the speed of a jack rabbit. With Pete Reiser at the plate, he promptly stole second. The Yankee manager, Bucky Harris, then had Bevens walk Reiser, even though Reiser represented the winning run.

Eddie Stanky was the Dodgers' next hitter, but Shotton substituted Cookie Lavagetto, a third baseman who was at his best with runners on base. Lavagetto came through with a double to right field which crashed high against the scoreboard. Bevens lost his no-hitter and the ball game.

The Yanks crushed the Dodgers 5-2 in the seventh game, and won the Series. Joe Page was the hero of that victory. He came in from the bull pen and pitched 1-hit ball for the last five innings.

A Yankee World Series hero, Joe Page, is congratulated by big boss Larry MacPhail (right) and teammate Joe DiMaggio (left).

123

45. The Pick-off

The records show that Bobby Feller was the hardest working pitcher of his day. He led the majors in the number of innings pitched for five years.

But Feller had the misfortune to play with the Cleveland Indians, a team that hadn't won a pennant since 1920. In 1948, however, it seemed that Feller and the rest of the Indians might finally have a chance to get into a World Series.

To do it, the Indians had to overcome two powerful opponents—the New York Yankees and the Boston Red Sox. These two teams were being kept in the thick of the fight by two of the best hitters in baseball—Joe DiMaggio and Ted Williams. DiMaggio hit 39 homers to lead the American League, while Williams won the batting title with .369.

Feller, Gene Bearden, Mike Garcia, and Bob Lemon were the backbone of the Indians' mound corps. The team's batting punch came from dark-haired Lou Boudreau, the shortstop and manager.

The American League flag race couldn't have been closer. The Indians and Red Sox ended in a tie. In a one-game play-off, Boudreau rocked Boston by batting two homers. The Indians won 8 to 3.

While the Indians fought their way to the flag in the American League, an interesting race developed in the National.

The St. Louis Cardinals had two players who took top individual honors in two departments. Stan Musial was the National League's leading hitter with 39 homers and a .376 batting average. His teammate, Harry "The Cat" Brecheen, was the best pitcher in the league with a 20–7 record.

Despite the great play of Musial and Brecheen, the Cards couldn't quite make it. For the Boston Braves had two pitchers who seemed unbeatable—Warren Spahn and John Sain. So regularly did this pair win that the Boston fans claimed the Braves could take the pennant all over again if the pitchers got sufficient rest. The formula, they said, was "Spahn, Sain and two days of Rain."

Manager Lou Boudreau warmed the hearts of ball fans everywhere by naming the hard-working Feller to pitch the World Series opener against Sain. The choice wasn't based entirely on sentiment. For although Feller had lost the booming fast ball that once enabled him to establish the all-time record of striking out 18 hitters in one game, he was still a mighty effective pitcher.

In place of the fast ball, Feller had developed one of the biggest and best curves the majors had ever seen. Above all, Boudreau knew Feller had a fighting heart.

As Sain and Feller dueled away, it seemed no one would score. The Braves' Phil Masi, however, got to second. As Feller "stretched" to pitch to Tommy Holmes, Masi took a long lead. Cleveland fans nudged each other.

"Watch this," they chortled. "Watch this!"

They were looking for the famous pick-off play that the Cleveland pitchers and Boudreau had used all season. Feller

Bob Feller faces batter Alvin Dark in the first game of the 1948 Series.

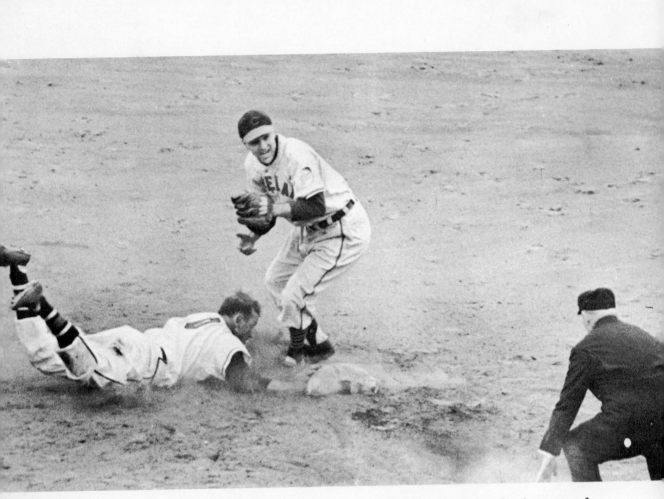

Lou Boudreau looks at the umpire with surprise as Phil Masi is declared safe at second.

took a quick look at Masi, then turned away. At that instant the pick-off signal had been passed. Boudreau dashed to second behind Masi. Feller whirled and threw the ball to him as Masi scrambled desperately to get back to the base.

"He's out! He's out!" the Cleveland fans yelled delightedly.

But no! The umpire had flung his hands sideward, palms down.

"Safe!" the hands signaled.

The call was hotly disputed then—and it still is today. The Braves' Tommy Holmes proceeded to get Masi home on a single, and Bobby Feller lost his first World Series game 1–0.

Although Feller lost the fifth game 11 to 5, the Indians won the sixth and final game 4–3 by dint of the fine pitching of Bearden and Lemon. They also won the Series.

It was Feller's last appearance in a World Series.

The Boston Braves had two pitchers who were almost unbeatable—southpaw Warren Spahn (left) and righty John Sain.

46. Casey

The Yankee management was unhappy about the team's third-place finish in 1948. To bring about a change, the club owners took the customary action. They fired manager Bucky Harris.

To the surprise of many, Casey Stengel was appointed to replace Harris. While Stengel had a good record as a manager of minor league teams, he had finished no higher than fourth in nine seasons as pilot of the Braves and Dodgers. When Casey joined the Yanks, many thought

him something of a clown. By the time he left, he showed that he was at least part genius.

Casey Stengel was schooled by such men as John McGraw and Wilbert Robinson. He knew the game as few know it even today. Unlike many old-timers, however, Casey stayed modern. He recognized that baseball had changed. It was a faster game played by faster men.

To keep his club at top strength, Stengel handled his lineup like a juggler. He

127

Into the air goes Manager Casey Stengel after his Yankees win their fifth straight American League pennant.

asked his men to play more than one position. Thus his batting order was never set; instead it shifted to meet the needs of each game.

Stengel's first season with the Yankees was difficult. He had to rebuild a badly weakened ball club. While he was doing so, his players came up with one injury after another.

Even so, the Yankees stayed close to the hot Boston Red Sox. On the last day of the 1949 season, the Sox were to play a double-header with the Yanks. The winner of both games would take the championship.

Ted Williams was having another good year. He led the League in homers with 43 and lost the batting title by but a fraction of a percentage point. The Sox' best pitchers—Ellis Kinder and Mel Parnell—were rested and ready for the Yanks. But the Yankees upset all the odds. They won the two games and the pennant.

The National League flag chase was just as close. Jackie Robinson, the League's best hitter, and pitcher Elwin "Preacher" Roe showed the way to a Brooklyn pennant. Victory wasn't assured until the last day of the season, though, when the Dodgers whipped the Phillies to nose out a hard-fighting St. Louis team.

The first two games of the World Series were as tight as the pennant races. The Yankees won the opener 1 to 0 on a homer by Tom "Old Reliable" Henrich. The Dodgers won the second game by the same score on a double by Jackie Robinson and a single by Gil Hodges.

But the Yankees won the next three to give Casey Stengel his first World Championship.

In the next ten years, Casey won nine more pennants and five more World Championships—a record difficult to beat.

47. Lightning Strikes Twice

While there have been many close finishes in big league competition, few will be remembered as long as the one that took place in the National League in 1951. For that was the year the New York Giants began a drive on August 11 to catch their bitterest rivals, the Brooklyn Dodgers. The Dodgers were leading by 13½ games at the time. The fact that Leo Durocher had abandoned the Dodgers to manage the Giants intensified the struggle.

Both the Giants and Dodgers played a torrid brand of baseball over the closing days of the season. Little by little, the Giants crept closer to the leaders.

On September 1, the Giants opened a two-game series against Brooklyn. At the time, they were riding a 16-game winning streak. The Giants won both games. Jim Hearn and Sal Maglie hurled masterfully for New York, while right fielder Don Mueller hit five homers to drive in almost all the Giant runs.

When the Giants and Dodgers met in a second two-game set a few weeks later, the Dodgers did a little better. They won one game. Then both teams made a western trip. During the playing, the Giants gained but one game.

The Dodgers, at this point, had 10 games to go. Five victories would mean the flag. But the Dodgers began to lose. And the Giants kept on winning.

In the last week of the season, the Dodgers were a half a game ahead with three games left. They had to win all three to cop the pennant. The Giants had two games with Boston left. To win the pennant the Giants had to hope for at least two victories and a Dodger loss.

The Dodgers' last three games were against the Phillies in Philadelphia. The Brooklyn nine lost their first game when Philly catcher Andy Seminick homered in the ninth inning. The Giants beat the Braves in the first of two.

This meant that Brooklyn had to win both of the remaining games with the Phillies to be sure of a tie. Don Newcombe, another Negro who followed the trail blazed by Jackie Robinson, took the mound for Brooklyn in the second game. He shut the Phils out 5 to 0.

The Phils bounced right back in the third and final game, getting off to a 6 to 1 lead after knocking out starter Preacher Roe. But Brooklyn fought gamely and managed to tie the score in the eighth. (At this point, word arrived that the Giants had again defeated the Braves.)

In the twelfth inning, Philadelphia loaded the bases with two out. First baseman Eddie Waitkus, a left-handed batter, drove a liner between first baseman Gil Hodges and second baseman Jackie Robinson.

Robinson, starting with Waitkus' swing, hurled his body to his left and speared the ball no more than an inch from the ground. It was probably the greatest catch of his career.

Thus the game remained tied in the thirteenth. At the top of the fourteenth, Robinson smacked out a homer to give the Dodgers the winning margin and a tie for the pennant.

129

Dodger pitcher Ralph Branca congratulates Giant hitter Bobby Thomson, the man who sent Branca crashing to defeat.

The thrills didn't end there, though. A three-game play-off was arranged, with the opener to be held at Ebbets Field. The Dodgers led with their ace right-hander, Ralph Branca. Branca went crashing to defeat when the Giants' Bobby Thomson cracked a two-run homer into the seats.

The Brooklyn team evened matters by taking the second game 10 to 0 behind pitcher Clem Labine.

Don Newcombe was the Brooklyn choice to oppose Larry Jansen in the dramatic "third" game. The Brooks quickly scored off Jansen and by the ninth inning were leading 4 to 1. Three outs and the game would be over. Brooklyn would be the champion of the National League.

But fate was taking a different turn. Shortstop Alvin Dark opened the inning

for the Giants with a single. He then went to third on another single by Don Mueller. Monte Irvin grounded out, but Whitey Lockman doubled. The Lockman hit scored one run, making the total 4 to 2. It also put runners on second and third and brought the winning run to the plate in the form of Bobby Thomson.

At this tense moment the Brooklyn manager made the fans buzz by replacing Newcombe with Ralph Branca.

"Doesn't he remember what Thomson did the last time?" one Brooklyn fan yelled.

"Yeah, but it can't happen again," another responded.

With the crowd tense and roaring with every move, Branca took his warm-up tosses. Finally he was ready. He stepped on the rubber, looked at the runners, and poured his fast ball toward the plate.

"Stuh-r-r-ri-i-ke!" the ump yelled.

The ball came back to Branca. The graceful right-hander rubbed it carefully, dried his fingers on the rosin bag, tugged at his cap, and then went back to the pitching plate. He took his stretch, again checked the runners, then fired to the waiting Thomson.

C-R-A-C-K!

The instant the bat hit the ball, the crowd knew. Called "the shot heard 'round the world," it was one of the most thrilling homers in baseball. It also proved that lightning can strike the same place twice.

Although the Giants had won 39 of their last 47 games to beat a strong Brooklyn team, they couldn't whip the Yankees in the World Series.

48. The Tape Measure Kid

Ball fans should never have doubted Casey Stengel's ability as a manager after the 1951 season. For though the Yanks were not as strong as either the Red Sox or the Indians, they managed to win the pennant.

The Yankees had two 21-game winners in Vic Raschi and Eddie Lopat. Allie Reynolds also pitched two no-hitters. But hitting was very weak. Only one player—Gil McDougald, a rookie infielder—hit over .300. There was another rookie, however, by the name of Lawrence "Yogi" Berra, who hit well when runners were on base. The stumpy, big-eared catcher had 88 "runs batted in" to lead the team.

The Yanks suffered most when Joe DiMaggio, their star center fielder, was in-

The old star and the new—Joe DiMaggio (left) poses with Mickey Mantle.

jured toward the close of the year. To replace him, Stengel daringly dipped into the Yankee farm system and called on a blond, converted shortstop. He was Mickey Mantle.

Actually Stengel had had his eye on Mantle for some time. Mantle had started playing professional ball two years before with a Class D club—the lowest classification in Organized Baseball. Mantle created quite a stir. Not only did he bat .313 for the year but he also knocked the ball over the fences whether batting right- or left-handed.

Promoted to a Class C team at Joplin, Missouri, the next year, Mantle hit .383 and had 26 homers.

Mantle's work was so promising that Stengel had him report to spring training with the Yankees in 1951. There it was discovered the youngster could not only hit, but had tremendous speed afoot as well as a better-than-average throwing arm. During the spring tour, the bull-shouldered youngster blasted the ball for such great distances that fans and sports writers couldn't believe their eyes. On one occasion, a smart publicist measured the length of a particularly long drive—it was well over 400 feet—with a tape measure. He wanted to make sure the writers wouldn't overlook Mickey's great power. Mickey's batting average during the tour was well over .400, too.

When Stengel added up all of Mantle's abilities, he came to the only conclusion possible:

131

"This boy will replace DiMag some-day."

Stengel kept Mantle with the Yankees during the early part of the season. He, DiMaggio, and Tommy Henrich worked with the boy on outfield play. But the switch from Class C ball to the majors was too much for the young speedster. The pitchers were so smart and so fast that Mantle lost all track of the strike zone. Stengel had no choice but to send him back to the minors—this time to Kansas City.

Mantle settled down quickly and soon was batting at a better than .300 clip. When injuries hobbled Joe DiMaggio, he got the call from Stengel:

"Come back to New York."

Mantle, still young enough to be chewing bubble gum, filled in ably for DiMaggio through the close of 1951. And when the Yankees met and defeated the Giants in World Series play, he made his first appearance in the great annual contest. He was to make many more in his remarkable major league career.

49. Beat the Yankees!

The New York Yankees have been the most dominant team in the history of baseball. But their long string of victories has not always made the baseball fans love them.

In fact they started winning pennants and World Championships so regularly they were criticized.

"No team should win that often," some said. "It's bad for baseball."

Soon fans and opponents alike developed a "beat-the-Yankees" attitude.

This feeling welled strongest in the breast of Brooklyn fans and players. For, although the Dodgers had won a few pennants, they had never been world champions. By the fifties, however, they were convinced they had the greatest team in the world.

When Brooklyn lost the play-off to the Phils in 1950 and the Giants in 1951,

Dodger fans repeated a cry that was to become a trademark:

"Wait till next year."

The Dodgers jumped away to a big lead in 1952. Then toward the end of the season the Giants began to close in. It looked like a repeat of 1951. But the Giant bench strength was thin, and the team fell back in the home stretch.

"Leave us at the Yankees!" the Brooklyn fans cried.

On paper the Yankees looked like the weaker ball club. Mickey Mantle, filling in nicely for Joe DiMaggio, and outfielder Gene Woodling were the only two players to hit over .300. Yogi Berra, however, again led the runs-batted-in department with 92.

To take the pennant, the Yanks had to fight off the Cleveland Indians with their powerful pitching staff of three 20-game

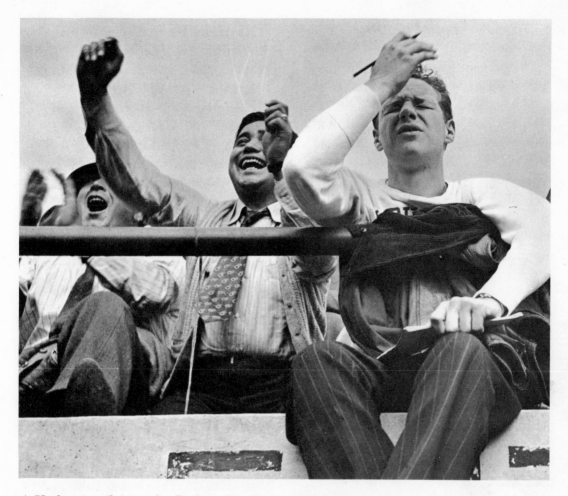

A Yankee fan (left) and a Dodger fan. Guess which team is winning.

winners—Early Wynn, Bob Lemon and Mike Garcia. They also had to overcome the Chicago White Sox.

Surprisingly, the Philadelphia Athletics caused some trouble, too. The A's had a tiny left-hander, Bobby Shantz, who won 24 games, while first baseman Ferris Fain became the League's leading hitter with a .327 average.

The World Series of 1952 went the full distance, but the Dodgers just couldn't bring the Yankees down, try as they might.

Again the old cry went up:
"Wait till next year!"

The next year arrived and the Dodgers' chances of winning a World Championship looked better than ever. They ran away with the National League pennant. At one point, the club won 41 out of 50 games. Carl Furillo, one of five regulars to hit over .300, won the National League batting title with .344.

Edwin "Duke" Snider, the Brooklyn center fielder, hit 42 homers. Catcher Roy Campanella hit 41 and played such a fine game through the season that he won the Most Valuable Player award for a second time. (He had previously been named in 1951.)

The Yankees, however, were stronger than the year before. They won the pennant easily, finishing in front by 8½ games. Lefty Edward "Whitey" Ford and Eddie Lopat won 34 games between them.

In one way, the World Series of 1953 reminded fans of the one played between the Cardinals and Tigers in 1931. For a man named Martin dominated the play. He was Billy Martin, the Yankees' aggressive second baseman. He hit two homers, two triples, a double, and seven singles as the Yankees took the Series in six games. Mickey Mantle swung a potent bat, too, driving in seven runs with five hits.

So the Dodgers had to say it again. "Wait 'till . . ."
Surely their day was coming.

50. A Change of Scene

Despite the superior brand of baseball that developed after World War II, many clubs lost money. There were several complex reasons for this. Although Americans had more leisure time than ever, there were more ways to spend it. Automobile travel increased as never before. Boating, golf, camping, bowling—all of these activities grew rapidly.

For a long time club owners ignored these challenges. They didn't seem to realize that many of the big league ball parks were in out-of-the-way places, that parking facilities were inadequate, and that population centers had been shifting.

Then, too, the Yankees, Dodgers, Red Sox, and Giants were beginning to dominate baseball. Interest in the weaker teams dropped rapidly.

By 1953 the club owners saw the picture all too clearly. Changes had to be made.

The first club to break away from the old league pattern was the Boston Braves. The team moved to Milwaukee, where they enjoyed an enthusiastic and profitable reception.

A new $5,000,000 municipal stadium was put at the Braves' disposal. The Stadium had 35,000 seats and plenty of parking space around it.

In 12 home games, the Milwaukee Braves drew more than 300,000 spectators. This topped the *total* 1952 attendance in Boston. Within a few years the St. Louis Browns moved to Baltimore and became the Orioles, while the Philadelphia Athletics shifted to Kansas City.

The fans adjusted to the changes nicely. They also seemed to welcome

A dejected Dodger, Roy Campanella, walks away from the plate after the Yankees' Hank Bauer (Number 9) chalks up the winning run in the sixth and deciding game of the 1953 World Series.

Two Giant heroes, Al Dark (left) and Willie Mays, lead a parade up New York City's lower Broadway to celebrate their team's 1954 pennant victory.

another change. The Cleveland Indians, behind the pitching of Early Wynn, Bob Lemon, and Mike Garcia, beat out the Yankees for the pennant in 1954.

To do it, the Indians had to win 111 games. This was eight more than the Yankees' victory total. It established a new American League record.

The New York Giants, meanwhile, made a marvelous recovery and took the flag away from the Dodgers. Two fine players—Willie Mays and Johnny Antonelli—gave the team the boost it needed to get past the powerful Dodgers.

Antonelli left-handed his way to 21 victories, while losing 7. Mays, just out of military service, was a tower of strength in the Giant batting order. The center fielder won the batting title with a .345 average. He also hit 41 homers and knocked in 110 runs.

Although not favored, the Giants easily won the World Series. The Indians didn't win a game.

All this represented a quick shift in the baseball scene. But it was only a brief one.

51. The Year That Was "Next Year"

Between 1939 and 1954, the Dodgers had won five pennants. Only once in that span did the team finish lower than third. But mighty as their efforts had been, the team hadn't won a World Series. Would 1955 be any different?

The season was barely under way when all of Brooklyn became convinced that 1955 was the year. For Brooklyn's Gil Hodges, Roy Campanella, Carl Furillo, and Duke Snider pounded out hits as never before. Although the Dodger pitching was weak, the thunderous attack launched by these four players carried Brooklyn to a smashing National League victory—13½ games ahead of the pack. Duke Snider knocked out 42 home runs and drove in 135 runs, the top record in the League. Roy Campanella added 32 homers and batted in another 100 runs. This performance won him his third annual award as Most Valuable Player in the National League.

Toward the end of the year Walter Alston, a new Brooklyn manager, apparently had an eye turned in the direction of the World Series, for he brought three young pitchers to the Dodgers from the vast Brooklyn farm system. These included right-handers Don Bessent and Roger Craig and a remarkable left-hander, Johnny Podres.

The Yankees were up to their old tricks in the American League. They staged a tough fight and finally won out over Chicago, Cleveland, and the ever threatening Boston Red Sox. Surprisingly the Yankee club boasted but two .300 hitters. One was Mickey Mantle, who batted .307. (Mickey also hit 37 homers.) The other was Bill "Moose" Skowron, a huge first baseman. Skowron batted .319. Yogi Berra, as usual, continued to hit the ball with runners on base, totaling 108 runs batted in. This gave him his third Most Valuable Player award.

While the Dodgers again seemed to have the better team, the opening World Series game followed an old pattern. The Yanks' first baseman, Joe Collins, banged out two homers, while little Whitey Ford and Bob Grim pitched the team to a 6–5 victory over Brooklyn.

The wailing of Brooklyn fans reached a new high, as the Yanks won the second game 4 to 2. Johnny Podres made them feel a little better by taming the Yanks 8 to 3 in the third game. Then the Brooks proceeded to win games four and five. Suddenly the Series score stood at Brooklyn 3 games, Yankees 2 games. One more victory and Brooklyn would have its first World Championship.

But cool, clever Whitey Ford kept up the suspense by beating Brooklyn 5–1. One game remained.

Johnny Podres matched his left-handed slants against the combined efforts of Bob Grim, Tommy Byrne, and Bob Turley in the seventh game. Brooklyn started the scoring in the fourth inning as Campanella hit a double, then raced home on a single by Brooklyn's fine shortstop, Harold "Pee Wee" Reese. Brooklyn scored again in the sixth on a

137

Five Dodger stalwarts (left to right): Duke Snider, Jackie Robinson, Roy Campanella, Pee-wee Reese, and Gil Hodges.

138

Campanella grabs Podres (center) in a bear hug after the last out of the last game of the 1955 Series.

After a breathtaking run, tiny Sandy Amoros plucks Berra's fly ball from the air.

single, error, infield out, and sacrifice fly.

The most sensational play of the Series cropped up in the bottom of the sixth with the Yankees at bat. Billy Martin walked, Gil McDougald bunted his way on. This brought Yogi Berra to the plate with the tying run.

Since Berra was a left-handed batter who liked to "pull" the ball into right field, the Dodger outfield shifted to right to meet this threat. Naturally the shift opened a big hole in left field.

Mr. Berra must have had his eye on this hole, for he promptly cracked a curving fly ball into it. Martin and McDougald, sure that Yogi's poke would be good for at least a double, flew around the bases.

To the roaring amazement of the crowd, however, the Dodgers' left fielder, tiny Sandy Amoros, raced to his right. And after a breathtaking run he reached out and plucked the ball from the air. Without hesitating, he whirled and threw to relay man Pee Wee Reese. Reese fired to Gil Hodges at first, doubling up McDougald and ending the threat.

That play seemed to be all the encouragement young Podres needed. He bore down with his crackling fast ball and teasing change of pace. The Dodgers won their first World Championship.

"Next year" had arrived at last.

52. The Classic

Many have wondered why baseball has fascinated Americans for so long. One answer is the element of suspense that's always present. Every inning, every game, and every season is different from the last.

The Brooklyn Dodgers' performance in 1956 is a good example of the unpredictable nature of baseball. That year the Dodgers boasted the most awesome batting power in the League and a fine crop of new pitchers.

But 1956 wasn't 1955. The team had to struggle mightily to stay in the race. Toward the end of the year, manager Alston looked for pitching help. He found it in Sal Maglie, the former Giant pitcher who had tied Brooklyn hitters in knots for years.

The Giants thought Maglie was "too old" and had sold him to Cleveland. But Cleveland didn't use Maglie much. When Brooklyn made an offer for him, the Indians were quick to accept.

Maglie turned out to be just what the Dodgers needed. He brought the Brooklyn team out of a tailspin late in September by pitching a no-hitter against the Pittsburgh Pirates. Meanwhile the Brooks scored five runs. From then on he gave the club just enough of a lift to enable it to squeeze past a young, hustling Milwaukee team on the last day of the season.

In the American League, Mickey Mantle won three batting titles—most homers with 52, most runs batted in with 130, and highest batting average, .353. This kind of slugging behind the fine pitching

of Whitey Ford (19–6) moved the Yanks to another pennant.

Thus the World Series stage was set just as it had been the year before. But would the players follow the same pattern?

Sal Maglie made it clear that the Dodgers intended to. He tamed the Yanks 6 to 3 in the opening game.

Don Larsen, a pitcher who didn't use a windup, started the second game for the Yanks. He did very well for a while as the Yankees built up a 6 to 0 lead. But the Brooklyn hitters let loose a barrage that ousted Larsen and six other pitchers. Score: Brooklyn 13, New York 9.

Whitey Ford and newcomer Tom Sturdivant hurled the Yanks to victories in the next two games. This evened the Series at two-all.

Casey Stengel then called on Larsen to pitch the fifth game—once more against Sal Maglie. Maglie, for his part, pitched well enough to win most ball games. He gave up two runs on five hits, one of them a homer by Mickey Mantle.

But Maglie's performance didn't match Larsen's. By the middle of the ball game, the crowd woke up to the fact that Larsen might pitch a no-hit, no-run game. In every inning he retired three hitters in a row. Jackie Robinson was the only man who came close to getting a hit. In the third inning, Robinson slammed a vicious drive at third baseman Andy Carey. The ball glanced off Carey's glove and bounced to shortstop Gil McDougald, who threw Robinson out easily.

The tension kept mounting as the game rolled on. It reached its peak in the ninth inning.

Carl Furillo was the first hitter Larsen faced. He was put out on a fly. Roy Campanella, the next hitter, grounded out. A pinch-hitter, Dale Mitchell, moved to the plate in place of Sal Maglie.

The crowd hushed as Larsen prepared to pitch. It was now obvious that all that stood between Larsen and a history-making record was the lone figure of Mitchell in a Brooklyn uniform.

"Ball one!" was the call on the first pitch.

Larsen rocked forward on the mound. His arm flashed downward.

"Stu-u-urike!"

Larsen kicked and fired again. Mitchell lashed at the ball and missed. It was strike two. Mitchell swung on the next pitch. This time he connected. The ball went foul.

The umpire threw a new ball into play. Larsen rubbed the slickness from the cover. He glanced about the diamond, took a deep breath, and stepped on the rubber.

In the next second the ball whizzed past Mitchell and banged into the catcher's glove.

"Strike thur-e-eee-e!"

With that emphatic call Don Larsen became the first man to pitch a perfect game in World Series competition. In doing so he threw but 97 pitches.

The Dodgers won the sixth game 1 to 0, but the Yankees soundly defeated them in the final contest 9 to 0. Once more the Yanks were world champions.

That winter the talk was not so much about the Yankee victory as it was about Don Larsen's classic. And well it should have been.

53. The Braves That Made Milwaukee Famous

When the Braves moved from Boston to Milwaukee, a great change came over the club. True, there were new faces in the lineup and there were new uniforms. But the change wasn't something that could be seen and touched. It was a change of spirit.

And no wonder. Some 2,000,000 Milwaukee residents a year gave the Braves the kind of support that is rarely found anywhere. The Braves responded gallantly, threatening the League leaders from the moment the franchise was shifted. In 1957 they made it all the way, winning the National League pennant.

Ageless Warren Spahn won 21 games, while Lew Burdette and Bob Buhl ably assisted him in holding enemy batters in check. Sparking the Braves' attack was the National League's Most Valuable Player for 1957, Henry Aaron. The slender outfielder led the circuit in homers with 44.

In the 1956 World Series, both Dodger Sal Maglie (upper left) and Yankee Don Larsen (bottom left) won pitching honors. But it was Larsen who achieved a remarkable no-hit, no-run game.

Red Schoendienst, Fred Haney, and Hank Aaron (left to right) are three of the Braves who helped make Milwaukee famous.

Like the Braves, the New York Yankees moved easily to the front and took the flag in the American League, although the White Sox were a threat most of the way.

Whitey Ford hurled the Yankees to victory in the opener of the World Series. The Yanks also won the third and sixth games. But the other four games went to Milwaukee. Three of the victories, as a matter of fact, were turned in by Lew Burdette. And they were impressive victories too, for Burdette hurled 24⅔ scoreless innings, close to an all-time record.

Henry Aaron was just as effective in the Series as he had been during the regular season. He collected eleven hits, three of them homers.

The new world champions made it clear that they intended to stay on top of the heap in 1958. They didn't have too much trouble with the usual contenders —the Dodgers and Giants—for these clubs had moved to the West Coast and were having trouble getting accustomed to new surroundings. The Dodgers, too, lost the services of their great catcher, Roy Campanella, after an unfortunate auto accident injured his spine and ended his career.

Surprisingly, the Braves had to hold off a spirited team of Pittsburgh Pirates. Once the Pirates were subdued, however, Milwaukee went on to win a second pennant for their new home town.

The New York Yankees easily outplayed every club in the American League in 1958. They built up an early lead and won the pennant without difficulty. Mickey Mantle again was the big gun for the Yankees, hitting 42 homers while building a .302 average.

As the World Series opened, the betting odds on the two teams were very close. They swung heavily to Milwaukee as the Braves won the first two games 4–3 and 13–5. Then the Yankees won the third game 4–0, but lost the fourth 3–0. At that point no one dreamed the Yankees any longer had a chance. For if the Yankees were to win the Series, it would be necessary to whip the Braves in three straight games. As for the Braves, they had to win but one of the three remaining games.

The end seemed to be in sight when the hero of the 1957 Series—Lew Burdette—was picked to pitch game number five. But the New York Yankees were a never-say-die ball club. They routed Burdette in that fifth game and won 7 to 0 behind fine pitching by Bob Turley.

The teams took the field in Milwaukee for the final two games. If the Braves won either one, of course, they would again be world champions.

The teams fought to a 2–2 tie in nine innings of the sixth game. In the tenth inning Warren Spahn gave up a homer to Gil McDougald. Two singles scored another Yankee run.

In the bottom of the tenth, the Braves scored one run and moved the tying run to third. But the Braves couldn't bring it across, and the Yankees won 4 to 3.

Now the issue was down to the seventh game. Burdette was on the hill for Milwaukee. Again the game went to a 2–2 tie. But Yogi Berra doubled, Elston

145

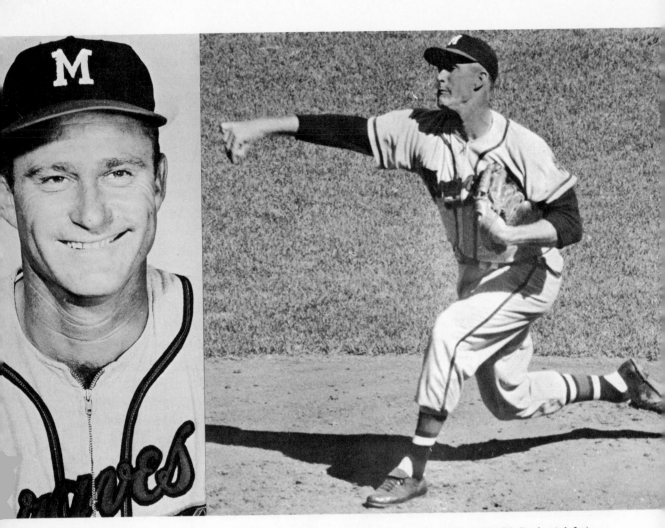

Smiling Lew Burdette (left). Pitching for the Braves in the 1957 World Series (right).

Howard singled, and Moose Skowron homered. The Braves couldn't match that outburst, and the Yankees regained the world title.

Although the Braves lost, one thing became clear. It wasn't just the brewing of fine beer that was making Milwaukee famous.

The city had a fighting, spirited ball club as well.

54. Fame and Fortune

When the Brooklyn Dodgers moved to Los Angeles, they set up camp in a huge oval stadium that was built to accommodate football crowds. A diamond was laid out at one end of the oval, and large screens were erected in the outfield. This arrangement was far from satisfactory to the ball players, and undoubtedly it had much to do with the club's finishing in seventh place in 1958.

But the Dodgers took new heart in 1959 and showed signs of wanting another slice of the World Series melon. During the early part of the season, they had to battle the Braves and Giants for the lead. Then in June the Pittsburgh Pirates showed that their second-place finish of the year before was no freak. It became a four-team race until September.

Suddenly the front-running Giants slipped to third and the Milwaukee Braves moved in on the Dodgers. On the last day of the season, the two clubs were tied. Shades of 1951!

In the best-of-three play-off series, however, the Dodgers quickly disposed of the Braves in two straight games.

While all this was going on, the Chicago White Sox finally beat out both Cleveland and the Yankees for the flag. It was the first time the Sox had won a pennant since 1919. They had finished third each year between 1952 and 1956, and second in 1957 and 1958

The World Series between the Dodgers and White Sox followed an old course—one unexpected thrill after another. The new Los Angeles Dodgers lost the first game 11–0, but went on to win the next three by scores of 4–3, 3–1, and 5–4. The fifth game, played in Los Angeles, saw White Sox star, Bob Shaw, beat the Dodgers' Sandy Koufax 1–0 in a tingling mound battle. But the Dodgers again became World Champions by winning the sixth game 9–3.

The most amazing performance of the Series was turned in by a 24-year-old rookie, the Dodgers' Larry Sherry. Sherry had joined the club in July. Although his minor league record wasn't too impressive, Sherry soon showed he could take it when the going was rough. He not only pitched well in the play-off series against the Braves, but he was also relief pitcher in each of the Dodger victories against the White Sox.

The Dodger's young shortstop, Charlie Neal, gave the club some unexpected batting punch. Although several pounds underweight as a result of the hot campaign, he collected ten hits, including two homers and two doubles.

Three oldsters—Duke Snider, Gil Hodges, and Carl Furillo—also came through in fine style for the Dodgers.

The Dodgers made history on the diamond, and they also made it at the gate by setting the following attendance records:

Club record—2,071,045
Single World Series game—92,706
Total World Series—420,784

If the Series had gone to seven games, the last figure, of course, would have been much higher. As it was, the Series meant a revenue of more than $5½ million.

The most astounding turnout of the season took place when 93,103 fans pushed into the Coliseum to see the Dodgers play an exhibition game against the Yankees as a tribute to Roy Campa-

The most amazing performance of the 1959 World Series was turned in by a 24-year-old rookie, the Dodgers' Larry Sherry.

nella. Some 15,000 were turned away.

For the Dodgers, 1959 was a wonderful year. It brought them fame and something new—fortune.

55. The Year the Kitten Purred

Since pitching is about 70% of a baseball team's strength, it isn't surprising to find that the top teams in 1959 had pitchers who made good showings.

Don Drysdale of the Dodgers, for example, led the League in strike-outs with 242. Sam Jones of the Giants pitched a no-hitter and had the National League's lowest earned run average. His teammate, Mike McCormick, also notched a no-hitter.

The champion White Sox' Early Wynn was on top with a 22-10 record in the American League. And Milwaukee's Warren Spahn and Lew Burdette each won 21 games.

The best pitching of all, however, was turned in by two Pittsburgh hurlers. One was Elroy Face. Pitching in relief, Face set a record by winning 18 games and losing but 1. He scored 17 of the victories consecutively.

The greatest single performance of the year was turned in by the second Pirate player, Harvey "The Kitten" Haddix. In a night game at Milwaukee, Haddix took the mound against Lew Burdette. Johnny Logan, the Braves' shortstop, was the only Milwaukee player to hit the ball with any force during the first nine innings. He drilled a shot to the right of the opposing shortstop, Dick Schofield, but Schofield made a good play on the ball and threw Logan out easily.

To end the ninth, Haddix struck out Lew Burdette. Like Don Larsen, he had pitched a perfect game up to that point. No walks. No hits. Twenty-seven outs in a row.

Although Pittsburgh had gotten several hits off Burdette, the Pirates couldn't score. The game went into extra innings.

Haddix was still effective in the tenth. Three men up, three down. The scoreless tie remained, however, and Haddix went back to the hill in the eleventh. Again it was three up and three down.

There was no scoring in the eleventh and twelfth innings, or by the top of the thirteenth, even though Pittsburgh had collected 12 hits off Lew Burdette. This meant Haddix had to go to the mound at least once more.

The first man to face Haddix in the thirteenth was Felix Mantilla. He hit a routine ground ball to third baseman Don Hoak. Hoak fielded the ball cleanly and threw to first baseman Rocky Nelson. But the throw was wild! It hit Nelson on the foot and Mantilla, safe on the error, became the first Milwaukee runner.

The crowd buzzed excitedly as homer king Ed Mathews moved to the batter's box. But the Braves were taking no chances on a double play by the Pirates. Mathews got Mantilla to second on a sacrifice.

To set up another possible double play, Haddix purposely walked Hank Aaron. This brought Joe Adcock to the plate. Haddix wheeled the first pitch plateward. It was a ball. The second pitch was in the strike zone. But only for an instant, for the powerful Adcock swung and drove the ball deep to center field. Fleet Bill Virdon raced after the drive, made a desperate last-minute

Harvey Haddix of the Pirates (left) and Early Wynn of the White Sox (right) also made baseball history in 1959.

lunge at the ball. He couldn't get it. The game was over.

Harvey Haddix, however, became the first man to pitch perfect ball for 12 innings. (Prior to Larsen, the only others to pitch perfect games had been John Richmond and John Ward in 1880, Cy Young in 1904, Addie Joss in 1908, Ernie

Shore in 1917, and Charlie Robertson in 1922.)

One other pitcher, Harry McIntire, came close to Haddix' performance. Pitching for Brooklyn against Pittsburgh, he eliminated every batter for 10⅔ innings. Then he lost the game in the thirteenth inning by a score of 1 to 0.

56. The Kubek Series

"The Pittsburgh Pirates are an extraordinary hodge-podge."

"No one can logically pick the New York Yankees to win the pennant."

These words were written by sports writers before the 1960 season began. Clearly, some felt, the Pirates and Yankees were not good enough to become League champions.

The Pirates, however, developed fine pitching, solid hitting, and a sound defense. Above all, the team never became discouraged. In early September, for example, the San Francisco Giants' left-hander Mike McCormick struck out 13 Pirates in a 6 to 3 victory. The next night Stan Williams of the Los Angeles Dodgers whipped the Pirates 5 to 2, again striking out 13 Pirates. Twenty-six strike-outs in two games!

But the Pirates bounced right back from these humiliating defeats, held off a fighting Milwaukee club, and won the National League pennant by seven games.

As for the Yankees, the team made the poorest start in its history. Only right fielder Roger Maris and first baseman Moose Skowron seemed to hit the ball well. The pitching was both good and bad. Still, by August Casey Stengel was able to move the club into second place behind the Baltimore Orioles. The Orioles, made up of a few oldsters and several players barely old enough to shave, looked like sure winners.

But something unusual happened in Yankee Stadium as Stengel's team seemed to be losing a double-header to the Washington Senators.

In the second game Mickey Mantle came to bat with Roger Maris on first. There was one out. Mantle slapped a double-play grounder to the infield. Maris, realizing he was out at second, slid hard into second baseman Billy Gardner to hamper his throw to first and "save" Mantle.

Suddenly, the crowd let out a gasp, a roar, then a lusty round of boos. As Maris crashed into Gardner, Mantle stopped running! And while Mickey trotted to the dugout, Maris lay writhing on the ground in pain, for Gardner's knee had caught him in the ribs.

"Quitter! Quitter!" the fans yelled at Mantle.

Stengel immediately yanked his prize player from the lineup.

Had Mantle really quit?

"No!" said Whitey Ford, Mantle's friend. He explained that Mantle thought there were two out when he went to bat and that when Maris was forced at second the inning was over.

Newsmen pressed Mantle for comment. But the slugger refused to say a word. The next day his bat spoke for him. He cracked two homers into the stands, each with a man on base, thereby driving in all the Yankee runs in a 4-3 victory.

From then on the Yankees picked up speed. They faltered once, dropping three games to the Orioles. But three weeks later they knocked the Orioles out of the race by sweeping a four-game series at Yankee Stadium. By the time it

The managers of opposing World Series teams—Danny Murtaugh (Pirates) and Casey Stengel (Yankees)—get together for a pre-game chat.

was over, Mickey Mantle, though injured, had hit 40 round-trippers to take the homer title for the fourth time.

"It's amazin' what he done," said Stengel. "And him a cripple playin' on one leg. He's been my most valuable player."

Although the pennant races had been astonishing enough, the World Series was even more so.

The Pirates brought down the Yanks 6–4 in the opener at Forbes Field. Second baseman Bill Mazeroski drove a two-run homer over the scoreboard in the fourth inning to highlight the Pittsburgh attack. The New York *Times* noted Mazeroski was "never regarded as a long ball hitter."

Mickey Mantle led the Yanks to a 16–3 victory in the second game by bashing two tremendous drives—one 400 feet and the other 450 feet—out of the park. When the Series switched to Yankee Stadium, the Yanks ripped into the Pirates, scoring 10 runs as Whitey Ford held the Bucs scoreless on four hits.

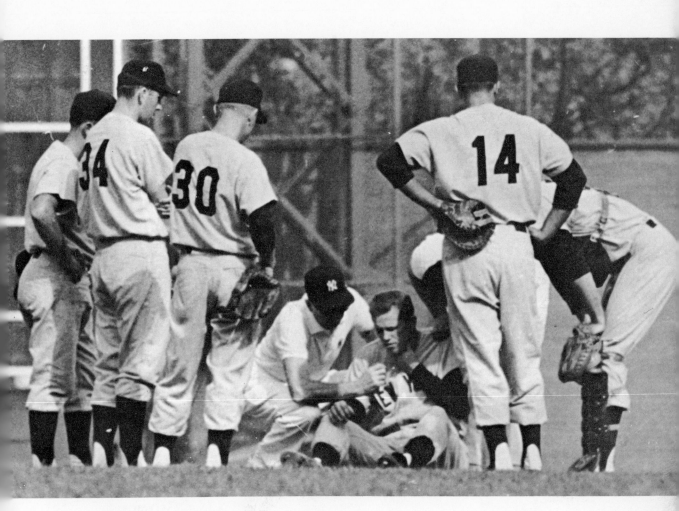

Tony Kubek, hit on the Adam's apple by the ball, is surrounded by anxious teammates.

After hitting the home run that gave Pittsburgh the 1960 World Series, a happy Bill Mazeroski cheerfully survives a champagne dousing from his fellow Pirates.

While no one was surprised to see Mantle hit his fourteenth Series homer in the fourth inning, all were stunned by the stick work of Bobby Richardson. The second baseman, with a height of 5'9" and weight of only 160 pounds, had a .252 average for the season and one homer to his credit. In the first inning, with the bases loaded, he cracked a homer ten rows deep into the left-field stands. A single in the fourth drove in two more runs to set a World Series record of six runs batted in for one game.

The Pirates seemed undisturbed by the ferocity of the Yankee attack. They won the fourth game 3–2 and the fifth game 5–2. This gave Pittsburgh a 3 to 2 lead

in games when the Series moved back to Pittsburgh for the finale.

In the sixth game the Yankees broke loose with another amazing hitting spree. While Whitey Ford shut the Pirates out on seven hits, the Yanks clubbed five Pirate pitchers for 17 hits and 12 runs.

The seventh game was a battle all the way. First the Pirates were ahead, then the Yankees. By the end of the eighth inning, the Yanks were leading 7–4.

Gino Cimoli was the first man up for the Pirates in the bottom of the eighth. He singled to right field. Bill Virdon then hit a sharp grounder to shortstop Tony Kubek. It looked as if it might be the start of a routine double-play. To the horror of the crowd, the ball took a freak hop and hit Kubek in the Adam's apple. He dropped to the ground in agony. It was an important play. Instead of two outs and the bases empty, the Pirates now had runners on first and second with none out.

Play resumed after Kubek was taken from the field and rushed to a hospital. The next Pirate singled, bringing in Cimoli for a score. A sacrifice moved the runners to second and third. An infield hit scored another run and still left two men on the bases.

This brought Hal Smith, catcher, to the plate. He promptly drove the ball high over the left-field wall. The Pirates had scored five runs and now led 9–7. But the Yanks didn't give up. They scored two runs in the ninth to tie the score.

The crowd stirred restlessly as the teams changed places. It quieted as Bill Mazeroski moved to the batter's box to face Ralph Terry, the Yankees' fifth pitcher. In minutes the ball game was over. Mazeroski hit Terry's second pitch over the left-field wall.

That shot gave the Pirates a 10 to 9 victory and the first world championship in 35 years.

Sixty-five records were set in the 1960 World Series, while twenty-seven were tied. But surely the bad bounce that hit Tony Kubek in the throat will be remembered longer than the records by Yankee fans.

The Yankee players, too, have reason to remember the "Kubek Series." For each member of the winning team received $8,417, which was $3,200 more than the losers collected.

57. The Retirements

Old age, the enemy of every man, comes early in the life of a ball player—usually between 35 and 40.

As the 1959 season ended, it looked as though two of the finest players of all time—Ted Williams and Stan Musial—had reached the end of the road.

Williams had batted but .254, the lowest in his career. He was 41 years old. Musial, too, had his poorest season, hitting .255. He was 39 years old.

But Williams and Musial were men of pride, determined to end their careers on a better note. Both decided to play in 1960.

For Musial it looked as if the decision had been a mistake. By May he was only hitting .250 as the Cardinals dropped to the second division. Manager Solly Hemus had no choice but to bench his star. Musial remained on the bench for a month, until called on to replace an injured outfielder.

By July Musial showed signs of recovering his form. Appearing as a pinch-hitter in an All-Star game, he blasted a long homer into the right-field stands. It brought the spectators roaring to their feet and kept them there for several minutes.

With that blow, Musial wrote some new facts into the record books. They were:

Most homers in All-Star games—Musial with 6.

Most total bases in All-Star games—Musial with 39.

Most at-bats in All-Star games—Musial with 57.

Most runs scored in All-Star games—Musial and Willie Mays of San Francisco with 11 each.

Musial's heroics didn't stop with the All-Star game. By mid-August he was batting at a .357 clip and had carried the Cards to within four games of the front-running Pirates. He finished the season with a .275 average, 17 homers, and 63 runs batted in.

It was such a remarkable recovery

In September of 1960, Ted Williams slammed out his last homer for the Red Sox—the 521st of his career.

that the Associated Press named Musial the "Comeback Player of the Year." He decided to play at least one more season.

Ted Williams started better than Musial in 1960. On August 11, in a game against Cleveland, The Splendid Splinter cracked two homers into the seats.

As the Red Sox flew to Baltimore, they broke training and drank a champagne toast to Williams. The two homers had moved him past Mel Ott, third among all-time homer hitters with 512.

Unlike Musial, Williams decided that the September 28 game against the Baltimore Orioles would be his last. Although the weather was bad, a good crowd had turned out to bid Williams farewell. When he came to bat for the last time in the eighth inning, the crowd stood and gave him a thundering ovation. Williams responded as only he knew how. He drove a 1–1 pitch into the Red Sox bull pen.

It was homer Number 521 for Williams, 13 less than second-place Jimmy Foxx. It was also 22 for the season and brought his average to .316 for 1960 and .345 for his career.

Williams, like Musial, was also given a "Comeback Player of the Year" award. And he deserved it.

Stories about retirements didn't end with the decisions of Stan Musial and Ted Williams.

Shortly after the World Series, photographers and reporters jammed into a room of a New York hotel. They listened in amazement as Yankee owner Dan Topping read a prepared statement that Casey Stengel's contract would not be

"I was told my services were no longer desired," Casey tells the reporters.

renewed. The Yankees, he said, had adopted an age-limit plan. Casey, at 70, was well beyond the limit.

Casey, grim of face, sat near Topping. For two hours he batted back the questions reporters threw at him.

"Were you fired, Casey?" one asked.

The lined face twitched. The old eyes glistened.

"Mr. Topping and Mr. Webb paid me off in full and told me my services were no longer desired because they want to put in a youth movement as an advance way of keeping the club going," Casey said. "That was their excuse—the best

they've got."

"But were you fired?" a reporter persisted.

"I was told my services were no longer desired."

"Are you sad about leaving the Yanks, Case?"

"It's not a sad occasion," Casey replied with a straight face. "I look very happy. Ha, ha."

And so the manager with the best record in baseball history left baseball's most successful team. But he would be back again with a new team in the 1962 season—the New York Metropolitans.

58. A New Home-Run Record

Baseball in 1961 was the same as it has always been—unpredictable. About the only thing the fans correctly anticipated was another Yankee pennant. But the Yankees were far from a shoo-in. For the Detroit Tigers provided the season's first big surprise by quickly taking the lead in the American League. (They had been picked to finish deep in the second division). They didn't yield first place until late July. And on September 1, when they traveled to New York for a three-game series with the Yanks, they were but a game and a half behind the first-place Bronx Bombers.

The Yankees, however, crushed Tiger dreams of landing in the World Series by taking the exciting and critical trio of contests by scores of 1–0, 7–2, and

8–5. These stunning victories seemed to spark the Yanks to even greater efforts. They won 13 more games in a row to increase their lead to 11½ games.

The Cincinnati Reds, also tabbed as a second-division team in the spring, upset the forecast by winning the National League flag. But the Reds were no match for the rampaging, hard-hitting Yankees in the World Series. They won only one out of five games. The scores were 2–0, 2–6, 3–2, 7–0 and 13–5. The Reds' lone victory featured a four-hit performance by the star of their mound staff, six-foot four-inch Joey Jay.

Jay's great pitching in the second game, however, was overshadowed by the hurling of the Yankees' Whitey Ford. Ford, who pitched the Yanks to shut-out

Pitcher Whitey Ford (left) and catcher Yogi Berra take a break during a Yankee practice session.

During the 1961 season two Yankee sluggers—Roger Maris (left) and Mickey Mantle—challenged Babe Ruth's home-run record.

Maris lifts his 61st homer of the season into the right field seats, thereby setting a record for a 162-game season.

victories in the first and fourth games, broke Babe Ruth's 43-year-old pitching record of 29⅔ scoreless World Series innings.

Ford passed Ruth's mark in the third inning of the fourth game. After retiring the first seven batters, Ford gave up a single to Darrell Johnson. But he got the next two outs on infield ground balls. He continued to add to his own record of scoreless innings until the sixth, when a foot injury forced his withdrawal from the game. As he left the field to a great crescendo of cheers from Yankee and Cincinnati rooters alike, the new World Series pitching mark stood at 32 scoreless innings.

There were all sorts of other records set in 1961. But the most exciting and most talked about involved baseball's most potent weapon—the home run. Play

had barely begun when the fans realized that the homer would dominate everything else that happened on the diamond. Players in both leagues were hitting homers as never before. When it was all over a total of 2,730 homers had been racked up, breaking the previous major-league record of 2,294 hit in 1956.

In the midst of all this activity, two men stood out. They were the Yankees' Roger Maris and Mickey Mantle. It soon became obvious that this brawny pair might accomplish what had never been done before. They might break the 60-homer record set by the incomparable Babe Ruth in 1927.

As the season wore on, a hot argument broke out among ball fans and officials. Baseball Commissioner Ford Frick and American League President Joe Cronin took opposite sides. The question involved these points:

Ruth's record was set in a 154-game season. The Yankees in 1961 were playing 162 games. If Maris or Mantle hit 61 or more homers after the 154 game mark was passed, would Organized Baseball say Ruth's record had been broken?

"Yes!" said Cronin.

"No!" said Frick.

Frick's ruling prevailed. The fans seemed to agree.

As each day slipped by, however, it looked as though Ruth's record *might* be broken within the 154-game period. By game 134, Maris had 53 homers, Mantle 48. At that same point, Ruth had belted out 49.

On September 14, however, Mantle conceded the odds were against him. He had gone hitless in seven at-bats in a double-header against the Chicago White Sox.

"I can't make it, not even in 162 games," he said glumly. With 53 homers to his credit by that date, Mantle would have to hit seven in the six games that remained on the schedule.

Maris, too, seemed to be losing ground. With 56 homers, he was one ahead of Ruth's pace for 148 games. But his last homer had been in game 142. Rugged Roger grimly continued swinging from the heels. In game 150, he hit his fifty-seventh homer; in game 151 his fifty-eighth. He now had tied the marks set by Jimmy Foxx in 1932 and Hank Greenberg in 1938.

Maris hit Number 59 during the 154th game. Ruth's record still stood. The fans settled back to see what Maris could do in the remaining games. Four games later he hit number 60. And on the last day of the season—before a roaring crowd at Yankee Stadium, Maris became the first player in major-league history to hit more than 60 homers "in a regular season."

Maris rapped out his sixty-first in the fourth inning of a game with the Boston Red Sox. Tracy Stallard, a 24-year-old rookie right-hander, was on the mound at the time.

There were other items of great interest in 1961. The two "old men" of the majors, Stan Musial and Warren Spahn, played brilliant ball and made it clear they would continue in 1962. The Phillies set an unenviable major-league record, losing 23 in a row. National League officials, in a historic three-and-a-half-hour meeting in Cincinnati, created two new teams—the Houston Colt 45's and the New York Mets. (Casey Stengel returned to New York as manager of the latter team).

But without doubt the great high point of that season was the Roger Maris feat. And yet, to many a nostalgic mind, the image of Babe Ruth as the King of Swat remained intact.

59. Dawn of Another Day

With the beginning of the 1962 season, baseball entered a new era. For the first time, the game boasted two major league circuits of ten teams each. The Colt 45s were playing in Houston, and in New York City the Mets opened their first season. In the American League, the Washington Senators moved to Minneapolis and changed their name to the Minnesota Twins. But the city of Washington formed another team with new players, a new manager, a new stadium, and an old name—the Washington Senators. Los Angeles entered the American League with the Angels, as well as building the new twenty-two-million-dollar Dodger Stadium in Chavez Ravine. Within the next few years, both Houston and the Mets were playing in brand-new stadiums, too; and in 1965 the Houston Colts changed their name to the Astros to match their amazing Astrodome. The Angels moved from Los Angeles to Anaheim, California, in 1966 and became the California Angels.

At first, it seemed that both leagues would profit from the expansion. By the close of 1962, for example, total attendance went well over 21,000,000, setting a new all-time high. The National League drew 11,360,159 fans, topping by some 200,000 an American League record set in 1948. In the following three years the total reached more than 13,500,000. In the American League, however, attendance dropped by almost 1,000,000 in 1963, steadied in 1964, then went down to 8,860,175 in 1965.

Something was lacking in American League play. It was competition. In 1962, for example, the Yankees won the pennant for the twelfth time in 14 years, finishing with a lead of five games. Although it was a narrow victory margin for the Yanks, there had been little doubt throughout the season that they would win. The next year the Yankees again captured the flag, this time by 10½ games. In 1964, when the Chicago White Sox ended the year only one game behind the Yanks, attendance picked up a little. But a year later the Minnesota Twins breezed to victory by seven games, and once again attendance fell off because of the lack of competition.

In sharp contrast to the American League, the Nationals staged a series of fierce battles among the first division teams during this period.

In 1962, for instance, the Dodgers were either at the top of the standings or tied for the lead for 111 days. But the West Coast club was under constant challenge—especially from the San Francisco Giants. During a long and successful home stand on July 27, the Dodgers beat the Giants three straight. But when Los Angeles visited San Francisco in August, the Giants won three straight. And when the season finally closed, the Giants and Dodgers were tied, setting the stage for the fourth play-off in the history of the League. In a best-of-three series, the Giants took the first game 8–0, lost the second 8–7, and won the third 6–4. In the World Series, however, the Giants bowed to

An Astrodome "Earthman" cleans the diamond before an exhibition game at Houston. Covered by a plastic dome, the unique, completely covered stadium is air-conditioned.

the Yankees in seven games.

The following year, National League fans were treated to another sensational finish. For almost three-fourths of the season, five teams were bunched at the top of the standings. In midsummer the Dodgers began to pull away from the other four. But just as it seemed certain that they would win the pennant and make up for the loss of 1962, the St. Louis Cardinals put on a spectacular drive, winning 19 out of 20. At the end of this spurt, the Cards were one game behind the Dodgers and about to engage them in a three-game set at St. Louis. Johnny Podres whipped the Cards 3–1 on three hits in the opener, while teammate Sandy Koufax won the next game 4–0 on four hits. In the third game, the Cards fought bitterly for thirteen innings, but finally lost, 6–5.

From that point on, the Dodgers had little difficulty nailing down the championship. Nor did their winning ways stop there. They humiliated the Yankees in the 1963 World Series by taking

The Reds' Chico Ruiz steals home with the winning sixth-inning run that started the Phils on their nine-game losing streak.

four in a row by scores of 5–2, 4–1, 1–0, and 2–1.

But if 1962 and 1963 were exciting years for National League followers, 1964 was even more so. And it provided one of professional baseball's strangest endings to a pennant chase.

Most of the excitement revolved around the Philadelphia Phillies, a club that had finished last in 1961, seventh in 1962, and fourth in 1963. By the middle of the following year, it began to look as if the Phils would win their first pennant since 1950. On September 21, when the Phils took the field against the Cincinnati Reds, they led the League by six and a half games with but 12 games remaining. A championship seemed a certainty.

In the sixth inning, the Reds' Chico Ruiz stole home with two out and the Reds' best hitter, Frank Robinson, at bat. This odd play beat the Phillies. But an even more bizarre fate was in store for them: they lost their next nine ball games!

While the Phillies were collapsing, the Cards, Reds, and Giants suddenly moved into contention. During the final three days of the season, the flag could have been won by any one of four teams. On the next-to-last day the Giants were eliminated. And on the last day the Cards and Reds were tied, with the Phils one game behind. The possibility of a three-way tie existed, but it ended when the Phillies whipped the Reds, 10–0, while the Cards beat the Mets, 11–5.

The rousing finish by the Cardinals did not end all the drama, for the Red

Cardinal third baseman Ken Boyer snares a foul hit by Yankee Roger Maris for the final out of the fifth 1964 World Series game. The Cards won, 5-2.

Birds then took on the Yankees in the World Series. The annual classic went the full seven games, with the Cards winning the championship for the first time since 1946.

The Cards failed to play like champions in 1965, however. By July they were in seventh place, eight and a half games behind the front-running Dodgers. But if the Cardinals were out of the competition, four other teams were not. By late August, the Giants were trailing the Dodgers by only a game and a half; the Reds by 2; Milwaukee by 4, and Pittsburgh by 4½. During the last exciting month, however, only the Giants were in contention. But San Francisco was not up to the task and finished two games behind Los Angeles.

The Dodgers, featuring a "ping pong" attack and a fierce running game, went on to beat the Minnesota Twins in the World Series in another seven-game set.

By the end of the 1962-65 period it was clear that the "balance" among the top teams in the National League attracted the attention of most fans. Still, serious questions were being raised about the eventual success of the expanded circuits. How long, for example, would fans remain loyal to ninth- and

Minnesota Twins shortstop Zoilo Versalles raises his gloved hand after making the tag on Dodger John Roseboro in the third inning of the sixth 1965 Series game. The Dodgers won the Series anyhow.

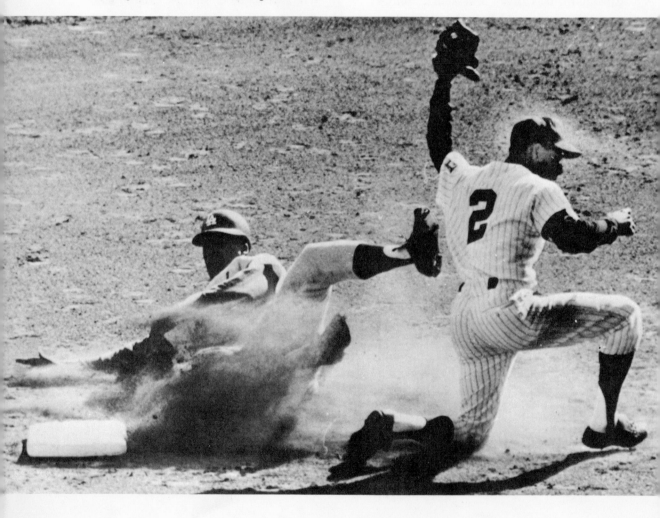

tenth-place teams that fell as many as 48½ games behind the leaders, as Washington did in 1963?

Only time, of course, would tell.

The pennant races were not the only events that made news as baseball's new era began to take shape. Other significant changes and activities included:

*The retirement late in 1963 of Stan Musial, the St. Louis Cardinals' great outfielder. As he ended his career in a game against the Cincinnati Reds, Musial collected two hits in three at-bats to pace the Cards to a 3–2 win. When the game was over, Musial had played in 3,026 games and batted 10,973 times. Credited with 3,630 hits, he had scored 475 homers, 177 triples and 725 doubles. His lifetime average was a remarkable .330.

*The purchase of the New York Yankees by the Columbia Broadcasting System in 1964.

*The perfect game Jim Bunning pitched on June 21, 1964, as the Phillies whipped the Mets, 6–0. It was the first such performance in the National League in 84 years and the eighth in the history of baseball.

*Johnny Keane's resignation at the close of the 1964 season as manager of the St. Louis Cardinals. His team had won the National League pennant and whipped the Yankees in World Series play. The Yanks promptly hired Keane to replace Yogi Berra, who moved over to the New York Mets.

*Milwaukee's sale of left-hander Warren Spahn to the Mets during the winter of 1964. Spahn had won 356 games in 20 years for the Braves. Released by the Mets late in 1965, he was picked up by the Giants.

*The Milwaukee Braves' announcement that the club planned to move to Atlanta.

*The retirement of Ford Frick as Commissioner of Baseball and the election of his successor, William D. Eckert.

*The second retirement of Casey Stengel, who had fractured his hip on July 25, 1965, five days before his 75th birthday. His decision ended a 56-year career as a player, coach, and manager.

*The death of Branch Rickey in 1965.

*Leo Durocher's return to baseball as a manager in 1966—this time at the helm of the Chicago Cubs.

50. The New Super-Stars

As baseball rolled into the 1960s, new "super-stars" emerged among the scores of highly skilled men who filled the rosters of various teams. These were players who somehow stood out above the others for their skill, courage, and durability—men who had much in common with the original Big Five of Ruth, Wagner, Cobb, Johnson, and Mathewson.

In the years following the expansion of the major leagues, three men clearly rated the designation of super-star—Maury Wills, Willie Mays, and Sandy Koufax. Mickey Mantle had surely deserved the title, too, in the late '50s and early '60s. But by the mid-'60s, a series of injuries had blunted much of his great talent and prevented his playing regularly.

Wills, one of the smallest players in baseball, played his first full season in 1960. That year he totaled 50 stolen bases. Although he dropped to 35 in 1961, he still led the National League. But Wills didn't begin to draw the full blast of national attention until 1962, when fans suddenly realized that he had a chance to break Ty Cobb's 47-year-old record of 96 thefts in one season. This became quite clear on September 7th, when Wills stole four bases in a game against the Pirates, thereby breaking the National League high of 80, set by Bob Bescher in 1911.

Wills kept right on swiping more bases, drawing closer and closer to Cobb's mark. This started a controversy very much like the Maris home-run feat of 1961. Would Wills get credit for a record if he stole more than 96 bases in 162 games?

As in the Maris case, Commissioner Frick ruled that the record—if there was one—would have to be on the basis of 154 games. By the time Wills completed the 154th game, he had stolen 95 bases. But a check of the records showed that, while Cobb had 96 for one season, that particular season had consisted of 156 games. Two games had ended in a tie and were later replayed. Wills, apparently unaffected by the controversy, kept the base paths hot. He stole his 96th and 97th in the Dodgers' 156th game, and by the close of the regular season he had a total of 100 stolen bases. During the play-off series with the Giants, he notched four more—three in the last game.

The Dodgers' Maury Wills holds up the base he stole for his 97th theft of the 1962 season, in a game against the Cardinals.

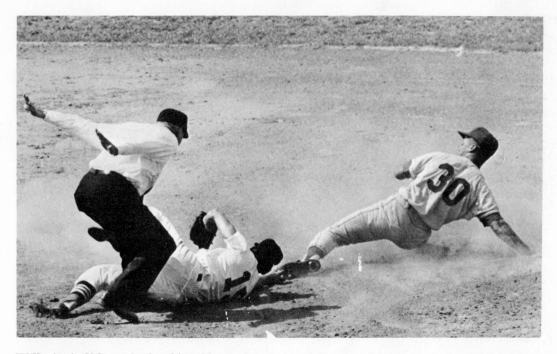

Wills (30) slides safe, hooking his toe into second base, as he safely steals the base in a 1962 game against the Houston Colts.

Early in the next season, Wills injured his foot. Still he managed to steal 40 bases, once again leading the National League. And even though the Dodgers dropped to a tie for sixth place in 1964, Wills paced the League by stealing 53 bases.

But Wills' total contribution to the Dodgers must be measured in many ways. As a switch-hitter who bunts well, hits to all fields, and has an excellent eye for the strike zone, Wills is an ideal lead-off man. In the field, he pulls in pop flies and ground balls like a vacuum cleaner. He has a good arm and is especially adept at the tricky business of tagging sliding runners.

Wills' specialty, however, is the ability to put enormous pressure on the defense. In game after game, he has bunted his way on base, stolen second

and sometimes third. Meanwhile, his nervous opponents have suffered from many dropped balls and overthrows.

Because of Maury's aggressiveness and inspired play, Manager Walt Alston appointed him captain of the Dodgers for 1965. Wills, responding to the honor, worked as never before, enjoying probably his best year. Although bothered considerably by a leg injury, he stole 94 bases and sported a .286 batting average, the highest in the Dodger club.

Willie "The Wonder" Mays seemed to reach a new and glittering status in the 1960s. For more than a decade he had been lashing the ball out of the park at decisive moments. And for more than a decade he had been making the impossible catch and the improbable throw. In addition, he always gave his all on the base paths.

169

By 1965 Willie Mays had led the League in homers four times with 51 in 1955, 49 in 1962, 47 in 1964, and 52 in 1965. He had captured the slugging title three times and had the highest batting average—.345—in the League in 1954. He had been in more than 2,000 ball games and during an 11-year period played no fewer than 150 games a season.

But it was more than Mays' record that impressed spectators. He was exciting to watch, especially when the chips were down. In addition, it was often obvious that Mays played on courage alone. In 1962, for example, he was the key man in the Giants' drive to the pennant. But on September 12 he collapsed from exhaustion. He missed the next three days. On the fourth day Mays was back in the lineup, his inspired play sparking the Giants to their tie with the Dodgers.

In the opening game of the play-off series, Mays cracked out two homers as he went 3-for-3. The Giants won the ball game, 8–0.

The following year, Mays' average was a dismal .245 by June 1. With typical determination, he battled out of his slump, ending the season with a .314 average. He also topped his mates with 103 RBI's.

Mays' popularity was illustrated on August 29, 1965, while the Giants were playing the Mets in New York. Mays had knocked in three runs in the third inning when he drove the ball over the wall in left-center field. That just about assured a victory for the Giants. Under normal circumstances, the fans might have started to leave. But in the eighth inning the Giants sent eight men to the plate, making it obvious that Willie would come to bat in the ninth. The crowd of 46,000 clung to their seats, hoping to see him hit another homer. This time, though, Mays grounded into a double play as he tried to check his swing. Immediately there was a mad rush for the gates.

Like Willie Mays, Sanford Koufax has given an extraordinary performance year after year. Twice he topped the League in wins, three times with the lowest Earned Run Average—the true mark of great pitching.

In 1962 the brilliant southpaw was at

Willie "The Wonder" Mays rounds third on his way home after blasting his 52nd homer of the 1965 season. He scored it in a game against the Cincinnati Reds.

his best for the opening third of the season. In April, he equaled Bob Feller's record of eighteen strikeouts in one game, and on June 30th he threw a no-hitter at the New York Mets. Soon after, however, he began to feel a strange numbness in his pitching hand. It started at the top of the index finger, spread to part of the palm and thumb. Koufax began to lose his effectiveness. In mid-July, with his record at 14–5, Sandy was put on the disabled list.

As the season drew to a close, the erratic, stumbling Dodgers were caught by the Giants. Although Koufax had rejoined the club on September 21, he had not regained his form. Still, Manager Alston asked Sandy to start the critical first play-off game against the San Francisco team. Before the end of the first inning, Koufax was in trouble. With two men out, Felipe Alou doubled and Mays followed with a homer. The first Giant at bat in the second inning hit another homer; the next batter singled. That was the end for Koufax.

The Giants, as previously stated, went on to win the play-off. Many "experts" argued, and probably correctly, that the flag would have been captured by the Dodgers if the strange circulatory ailment had not numbed Sandy's finger.

Sandy recovered his form in 1963 and was the outstanding pitcher in baseball. He had a 25–5 record and an Earned Run Average of 1.88. Eleven of Sandy's victories were shutouts, one a no-hitter over the Giants. In addition, he beat the Yankees twice in the Dodgers' four-game sweep of the World Series. In the first game, Sandy struck out 15 for

The Dodgers' ace pitcher in top form.

a new Series record.

Although hampered by two serious injuries in 1964 and forced to withdraw before the close of the campaign, Koufax still managed to compile a 19–5 record and the League's lowest Earned Run Average, which was 1.74. He also ranked first among National League pitchers in the number of shutouts—seven.

Early in 1965, the Koufax career appeared to be over. His pitching arm was swollen and throbbed with pain. He had become a victim of arthritis, a disease that cripples the joints. But his arm responded to treatment and Sandy went on to enjoy perhaps his best season. On September 9th at Los Angeles, for example, he pitched a perfect 1–0 game against the Cubs. That night he also became the first player to pitch four no-hitters during his career. The 29-year-old fireballer struck out 14, including the last 6 batters he faced.

On September 29, Koufax shut out the Reds, 5–0, on two hits. In this contest, he struck out 13. Two days later, against the Milwaukee Braves, Koufax again struck out 13. He allowed only four hits as the Dodgers won the game, 3–1, as well as the National League flag.

By the end of the regular season, Sandy had won 26 and lost eight. He had also set a major league record of 382 strikeouts. His string of shutouts ran to eight and, as the Dodgers made their stretch drive, he gave up but one run in his last three starts.

The World Series opened on October 6, which Sandy observed as a religious holiday. As a result, Don Drysdale, who had had a wonderful season, got the assignment to pitch the opener against Minnesota. The Dodgers lost 8–6, but Sandy was expected to even the Series the next day. Although Koufax pitched well, he was behind 2–1, when lifted for a pinch hitter in the seventh. Sandy's removal caused one wag to remark: "Well, at least he's human."

Claude Osteen and Drysdale hurled the Dodgers to victory in the next two games and, with the Series tied at two all, Walter Alston called on Koufax again. Sandy was rarely better as he pitched the Dodgers to a 7–0 victory. He allowed but four hits.

The driving Minnesota Twins, behind the great hurling of Jim "Mudcat" Grant and the sparkling play of Zoilo Versalles, again defeated the Dodgers in the sixth game, this time 5–1. Thus the stage was set for another drama starring Sandy Koufax.

Koufax, pitching again after two days' rest, had difficulty with his control in the early part of the game, but he managed to hold the straining Twins scoreless. In the fourth inning, outfielder Lou Johnson, a key player in the Dodger pennant chase, hit a homer. A double and a single scored another run.

The 2–0 lead looked extremely slim in the fifth inning. Frank Quilici lined a double off the left-field fence. Pinch-hitter Rich Rollins walked. Thus the tying runs were on base with only one out and the top of the Minnesota batting order coming to the plate.

Versalles, an always dangerous hitter, lashed what appeared to be a sure double down the third base line. But aging Jim Gilliam, who had come out of retirement as a coach to help the Dodgers, back-handed the drive and stepped on third. The next hitter hit into a force-out.

Koufax' control improved and he continued to smother the Twins' attack. In the ninth, Harmon Killebrew lined a single to left with one out. A home run, of course, would mean a tie. But Koufax struck out the next two hitters.

The New York *Times* referred to Sandy's performance in 1965 as an "incredible personal accomplishment." It surely was.

The Super-stars, of course, don't play forever. As fans looked forward to the late 60s and early 70s, they began to wonder who would earn the title next.

61. The New Amateurs

Soon after the professionals took over the National Association in 1871, the amateur game—at least as it was known then—began to disappear. For almost half a century, organized play among amateurs was limited to high school and college teams.

In the mid-twenties, however, the American Legion, prompted by the late Major John L. Griffith, launched a new movement—baseball leagues for boys. This movement spread and other national organizations—American Baseball Congress in 1935 and Little League in 1939—began to crop up.

Following World War II, amateur baseball programs boomed at a fantastic rate. New national groups, like the Babe Ruth and Pony and Colt leagues, gave amateur ball a big push. So did thousands of community organizations and "service" clubs, such as Optimist International, Rotary, and Kiwanis.

Since the mid-thirties, high school baseball has experienced a great revival. More high schools now sponsor baseball than any other sport with the exception of basketball and track and field. The college program, too, has expanded rapidly.

The number of players linked to national organizations alone jumped from 5,000,000 in 1942 to about 7,000,000 in 1961. In addition it is estimated that some 3,000,000 players are connected with teams having no affiliation with the national groups.

The amateur game—which accommodates players from age eight through manhood—also has gone abroad. By 1961, for example, more than 1,300 teams were affiliated with the Babe Ruth League. Almost 200 of these were located in 14 foreign countries—Belgium, Italy, Morocco, Spain, and others. Little League also has scores of affiliate teams in other countries.

In many ways, the programs of the national organizations are patterned after the professional game. Players are uniformed, play on manicured diamonds, and sit in dugouts. At the season's end, there is a "World Series," which often receives wide publicity. In 1960, for instance, the Little·League finals were televised nationally and broadcast by 126 stations.

Like the Atlantics, Washington Nationals, and Eckfords of the 1860s, the amateurs of today—although considerably younger—have many problems. Luckily these are gradually being licked by intelligent and responsible people.

Most of the adults who run amateur programs (exclusive of school programs) are volunteer workers, while the remainder receive a small hourly wage, or belong to public recreation staffs.

For the most part, the sizable funds needed for field maintenance, uniforms, bats, balls, bases, etc., come from voluntary local contributions. Some of the national organizations, however, receive monetary support from Organized Baseball and some of the larger industrial firms.

173

Grenshaw Owens, catcher from Jeffersonville, Indiana, slides safely into home under the feet of Takayuki Saito from Tokyo, Japan, in the second inning of a 1965 Little League World Series game.

The new amateurs have given many players a big push toward stardom in the Big Leagues. Roger Maris and Bill Skowron of the Yankees, Joey Jay of the Cincinnati Reds, and Milt Pappas and Jack Fisher of the Baltimore Orioles are good examples.

The impact of this group goes deeper than that, however. Despite the critics, "kid baseball" has become an important and growing part of social life in the United States. There are those, too, who will argue that the new amateurs represent the biggest development in the sports world in years.

With more than 10,000,000 involved in amateur baseball and well over 35,-000,000 attending professional games each year, one might raise this question:

What is it about baseball that appeals so strongly to fans and participants, especially the American fan and participant?

While it is always dangerous to generalize about any subject, many baseball-minded people agree on the following as at least a partial answer:

Although baseball is a game, it illustrates over and over again that, when one is striving to accomplish something, he must never give up until the issue is settled. (You're not licked till the last man is out, the ball player says.)

Baseball demands the best possible *individual* performance as well as a top *team* effort.

The complexity of the game tests one's wits and judgement.

Baseball is a healthful, clean, and exciting sport that requires not only great skill, but a great number of skills.

In short, many believe that baseball teaches many lessons that have parallels in real life and, further, that the game reflects much of what makes every American tick.

Regardless of whether the reader subscribes to these theories, it seems a certainty that as long as there is a United States of America, there will be a game called baseball. The National Pastime is here to stay.

Baseball's Hall of Fame

When the Mills Commission said Abner Doubleday invented baseball in Cooperstown, New York, it did more than climax a boiling argument. It planted an idea in the minds of a number of Cooperstown residents.

"If Cooperstown has been picked as the birthplace of baseball, why don't we build a memorial to the game?" these people asked.

A dozen years after release of the Mills report, a group of public-spirited Cooperstown folk made a modest start. They leased the "Phinney lot," the piece of property off Main Street which Abner Graves had identified as a possible site of the first baseball game.

Then the local residents cleared the field, laid out a diamond, and built a set of bleachers. In September of 1920, the park was dedicated as "Doubleday Field." Only one major baseball figure attended the ceremony—John Heydler, president of the National League.

Later, Cooperstown bought the field and raised funds to improve it.

Unfortunately for many years baseball club owners and officials didn't know what was going on in Cooperstown. But luckily a wealthy Cooperstown man, Stephen Carlton Clark, became interested in collecting baseball exhibits. He and others in Cooperstown felt the exhibits should be put on display with new ones added each year. Clark sought out Ford Frick, then president of the National League, and asked for help.

Frick was very enthusiastic about Clark's proposal for a national museum. He even expanded on the idea.

"Why not establish a baseball Hall of Fame?" he asked.

Soon the plans were laid.

In 1936 the Baseball Writer's Association elected the first five members to the Hall of Fame. They included Ty Cobb, Christy Mathewson, Honus Wagner, Babe Ruth, and Walter Johnson. The writers had made a good choice. Without doubt, these were the *Big Five* of baseball.

Subsequently Clark contributed the money for a building to house the memorial. The building was opened amid much pomp and ceremony on June 12, 1939, one hundred years after Doubleday had supposedly originated the game of baseball.

Scores of important baseball personalities —including Cobb, Wagner, Ruth and Johnson—were on hand as Judge Landis made his dedication speech from a little platform in front of the building.

Today the baseball shrine is double its original size. The basement and four floors of the museum contain a huge collection of baseball mementos—everything from Ty Cobb's sliding pads, to the lockers and uniforms used by Babe Ruth and Walter Johnson.

While Organized Baseball originally gave no financial support to the memorial, it now makes a substantial annual cash contribution toward the upkeep. It also arranges for a National League team to play an American League team on Doubleday Field each year.

The Hall of Fame is located in a separate wing of the building. The room is rectangular with a high ceiling. The plaques for the members rest in alcoves along the walls. And below is a list of the names to be found there—honored by thousands of devoted baseball fans:

1936   Tyrus Raymond Cobb
1936   George Herman "Babe" Ruth
1936   Christopher Mathewson
1936   John P. "Honus" Wagner
1936   Walter Perry Johnson
1937   Denton T. "Cy" Young
1937   George Wright
1937   Tristram E. "Tris" Speaker

1937	John J. McGraw	1948	Herbert J. Pennock
1937	Cornelius McGillicuddy (Connie Mack)	1949	Charles A. "Kid" Nichols
		1949	Charles L. Gehringer
1937	Napoleon "Larry" Lajoie	1949	Mordecai Peter Brown
1937	Byron Bancroft Johnson	1951	Melvin T. Ott
1937	Morgan G. Bulkeley	1951	James E. Foxx
1938	Henry Chadwick	1952	Paul G. Waner
1938	Albert Joy Cartwright, Jr.	1952	Harry E. Heilmann
1938	Grover Cleveland Alexander	1953	William H. "Harry" Wright
1939	Albert Goodwill Spalding	1953	Roderick J. "Bobby" Wallace
1939	George Harold Sisler	1953	Aloysius H. Simmons
1939	Charles Radbourn	1953	William J. Klem
1939	William H. Keeler	1953	Jay Hanna "Dizzy" Dean
1939	Henry Louis Gehrig	1953	Thomas H. Connolly
1939	William B. "Buck" Ewing	1953	Charles A. "Chief" Bender
1939	W. A. "Candy" Cummings	1953	Edward G. Barrow
1939	Charles A. Comiskey	1954	William H. Terry
1939	Edward Trowbridge Collins	1954	Walter J. "Rabbit" Maranville
1939	Adrian Constantine Anson	1954	William M. Dickey
1942	Rogers Hornsby	1955	Arthur C. "Dazzy" Vance
1944	Kenesaw Mountain Landis	1955	Raymond W. Schalk
1945	Wilbert Robinson	1955	Theodore A. Lyons
1945	James H. O'Rourke	1955	Charles Leo "Gabby" Hartnett
1945	Michael J. "King" Kelly	1955	Joseph P. DiMaggio
1945	Hugh A. Jennings	1955	John F. "Home Run" Baker
1945	Hugh Duffy	1956	Henry B. Greenberg
1945	Edward J. Delehanty	1956	Joseph E. Cronin
1945	James J. Collins	1957	Joseph V. McCarthy
1945	Frederick C. Clarke	1957	Samuel E. Crawford
1945	Dennis Brouthers	1959	Zachariah D. Wheat
1945	Roger P. Bresnahan	1961	William R. Hamilton
1946	Edward Arthur Walsh	1961	Max G. Carey
1946	George Edward Waddell	1962	Jack R. Robinson
1946	Joseph B. Tinker	1962	Robert W. Feller
1946	Edward S. Plank	1962	William B. McKechnie
1946	Joseph Jerome McGinnity	1962	Edd J. Roush
1946	Thomas F. McCarthy	1963	Eppa Rixey
1946	Clark C. Griffith	1963	Edgar "Sam" Rice
1946	John Joseph Evers	1963	Elmer Flick
1946	John Dwight Chesbro	1963	John Clarkson
1946	Frank LeRoy Chance	1964	Luke Appling
1946	Jesse C. Burkett	1964	Urban "Red" Faber
1947	Carl O. Hubbell	1964	Heinie Manush
1947	Robert Moses Grove	1964	John Montgomery Ward
1947	Frank F. Frisch	1964	Miller Huggins
1947	Gordon S. "Mickey" Cochrane	1964	Tim Keefe
		1964	Burleigh Grimes
1948	Harold J. "Pie" Traynor	1965	James "Pud" Galvin
		1966	Theodore Samuel "Ted" Williams
		1966	Charles Dillon "Casey" Stengel

Below is a list of pennant winners, beginning in 1901. The number of World Series games won and lost appears after the name of the winner. If no score is given, no Series was played that year.

American League	Year	National League
Chicago	1901	Pittsburgh
Philadelphia	1902	Pittsburgh
Boston 5–3	1903	Pittsburgh
Boston	1904	New York
Philadelphia	1905	New York 4–1
Chicago 4–2	1906	Chicago
Detroit	1907	Chicago 4–0; 1 tie
Detroit	1908	Chicago 4–1
Detroit	1909	Pittsburgh 4–3
Philadelphia 4–1	1910	Chicago
Philadelphia 4–2	1911	New York
Boston 4–3; 1 tie	1912	New York
Philadelphia 4–1	1913	New York
Philadelphia	1914	Boston 4–0
Boston 4–1	1915	Philadelphia
Boston 4–1	1916	Brooklyn
Chicago 4–2	1917	New York
Boston 4–2	1918	Chicago
Chicago	1919	Cincinnati 5–3
Cleveland 5–2	1920	Brooklyn
New York	1921	New York 5–3
New York	1922	New York 4–0; 1 tie
New York 4–2	1923	New York
Washington 4–3	1924	New York
Washington	1925	Pittsburgh 4–3
New York	1926	St. Louis 4–3
New York 4–0	1927	Pittsburgh
New York 4–0	1928	St. Louis
Philadelphia 4–1	1929	Chicago
Philadelphia 4–2	1930	St. Louis
Philadelphia	1931	St. Louis 4–3
New York 4–0	1932	Chicago
Washington	1933	New York 4–1
Detroit	1934	St. Louis 4–3
Detroit 4–2	1935	Chicago
New York 4–2	1936	New York
New York 4–1	1937	New York
New York 4–0	1938	Chicago
New York 4–0	1939	Cincinnati
Detroit	1940	Cincinnati 4–3
New York 4–1	1941	Brooklyn
New York	1942	St. Louis 4–1
New York 4–1	1943	St. Louis
St. Louis	1944	St. Louis 4–2
Detroit 4–3	1945	Chicago
Boston	1946	St. Louis 4–3
New York 4–3	1947	Brooklyn

American League	Year	National League
Cleveland 4-2	1948	Boston
New York 4-1	1949	Brooklyn
New York 4-0	1950	Philadelphia
New York 4-2	1951	New York
New York 4-3	1952	Brooklyn
New York 4-2	1953	Brooklyn
Cleveland	1954	New York 4-0
New York	1955	Brooklyn 4-3
New York 4-3	1956	Brooklyn
New York	1957	Milwaukee 4-3
New York 4-3	1958	Milwaukee
Chicago	1959	Los Angeles 4-2
New York	1960	Pittsburgh 4-3
New York 4-1	1961	Cincinnati
New York 4-3	1962	San Francisco
New York	**1963**	Los Angeles 4-0
New York	1964	St. Louis 4-3
Minnesota	1965	Los Angeles 4-3

Pitchers since 1900 who have won 300 or more games

Denton Young	511	Warren Spahn	359
Walter Johnson	416	Eddie Plank	324
Christy Mathewson	373	Robert Grove	300
Grover Alexander	373	Early Wynn	300
Charles Nichols	360		

Players since 1900 who have hit 300 or more home runs

Babe Ruth	714	Ralph Kiner	369
Jimmy Foxx	534	Joe DiMaggio	361
Ted Williams	521	Johnny Mize	359
Mel Ott	511	Yogi Berra	358
Willie Mays	505	Hank Greenberg	331
Lou Gehrig	493	Rocky Colavito	328
Ed Mathews	477	Frank Robinson	324
Stan Musial	475	Joseph Adcock	318
Mickey Mantle	473	Roy Sievers	318
Duke Snider	407	Al Simmons	307
Ernie Banks	404	Rogers Hornsby	302
Henry Aaron	398	Chuck Klein	300
Gil Hodges	370		

Players between 1900 and 1963 who have hit .400 or better in one season

Rogers Hornsby	.424 in 1924	Ted Williams	.406 in 1941
Larry Lajoie	.422 in 1901	Rogers Hornsby	.403 in 1925
George Sisler	.420 in 1922	Harry Heilmann	.403 in 1923
Ty Cobb	.420 in 1911	Rogers Hornsby	.401 in 1922
Ty Cobb	.410 in 1912	Bill Terry	.401 in 1930
Joseph Jackson	.408 in 1911	Ty Cobb	.401 in 1922
George Sisler	.407 in 1920		

Players who have hit 50 or more home runs in one season between 1900 and 1965

162-game season

Roger Maris—61 in 1961 Mickey Mantle—54 in 1961 Willie Mays—52 in 1965

Record for 154-game season

Babe Ruth—60 in 1927   Ralph Kiner—54 in 1949
Babe Ruth—59 in 1921   Mickey Mantle—52 in 1956
Jimmy Foxx—58 in 1932   Ralph Kiner—51 in 1947
Hank Greenberg—58 in 1938   Johnny Mize—51 in 1947
Lewis Wilson—56 in 1930   Willie Mays—51 in 1955
Babe Ruth—54 in 1920   Jimmy Foxx—50 in 1938
Babe Ruth—54 in 1928

Major League Club Rosters

National League	*American League*
Atlanta Braves	Baltimore Orioles
Chicago Cubs	Boston Red Sox
Cincinnati Reds	California Angels
Houston Astros	Chicago White Sox
Los Angeles Dodgers	Cleveland Indians
New York Mets	Detroit Tigers
Philadelphia Phillies	Kansas City Athletics
Pittsburgh Pirates	Minnesota Twins
San Francisco Giants	New York Yankees
St. Louis Cardinals	Washington Senators

Index

184